# TRUE TALES OF THE
# MACABRE
# WITHIN SIGHT
# OF THE GIBBET

A TALE OF MURDER, HIGHWAY ROBBERY AND
TRANSPORTATION IN THE PEAK DISTRICT

T0326059

# ABOUT THE AUTHOR

Ian Morgan was born in Chesterfield and has lived locally all his life. From an early age he became captivated by the intrigues and history of England's colourful past, its many historic buildings and notable characters, as well as having an extensive knowledge of crime and punishment from times past. He is a published author on historical subjects and has made many appearances on radio in that context. These include articles for BBC Sheffield, BBC Lincolnshire, BBC Nottingham and BBC Derby as well as independent radio.

Not only does he enjoy giving guided walks around historical locations, but he also spends much of his time travelling the country giving illustrated talks and lectures to a wide range of audiences. It was while researching the causes and consequences of the plague, and in particular its effect on the village of Eyam in Derbyshire, that he first encountered the tale of Anthony Lingard – the last man to be gibbeted in Derbyshire. Realising that the Lingard story would be an ideal follow-up book to his earlier short story *Tom Otter and the Slaying of Mary Kirkham*, he decided to put his other projects to one side for a while. Extensive and detailed research has led to the telling of a remarkable story, one of brutality, hardship and endurance.

Ian's idea of having a rest is to give his time to English Heritage to act as a guide at a number of their properties, most notably Bolsover Castle in Derbyshire where both he and his colleagues are proud to say they provide an experience that truly enhances visitor enjoyment. He is married to Angela and together they have three children. They currently live close to the Nottinghamshire-Derbyshire border surrounded by its many parks and stately homes.

# TRUE TALES OF THE
# MACABRE
# WITHIN SIGHT
# OF THE GIBBET

A TALE OF MURDER, HIGHWAY ROBBERY AND
TRANSPORTATION IN THE PEAK DISTRICT

## IAN MORGAN

DB
PUBLISHING

# DEDICATION

*For Natalie, Charlotte and Lee*

First published in Great Britain in 2009 by The Breedon Books Publishing Company Limited, Breedon House, 3 The Parker Centre, Derby, DE21 4SZ

This edition published in Great Britain in 2012 by The Derby Books Publishing Company Limited, 3 The Parker Centre, Derby, DE21 4SZ.

ISBN 978-1-78091-170-0

Printed and bound by Copytech (UK) Limited, Peterborough.

# CONTENTS

The Lingard Family Tree      6

Acknowledgements      7

Definitions      8

Introduction      9

Preparing the Way      16

The Workhouse Boy      32

Litton Mill      50

The Toll House Murder      70

Trial and Execution      78

A Warning to Others      91

Hannah Bocking      100

Within Sight of the Gibbet      113

Exile      126

The Defiant One      144

Hell in Paradise      157

Afterwards      179

Appendix A      192

Appendix B      196

Appendix C      199

Appendix D      200

Appendix E      202

Notes      204

Bibliography      205

# LINGARD FAMILY TREE

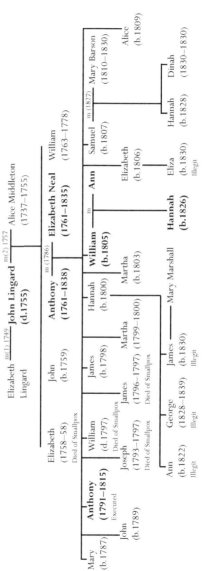

The Lingard Family tree with the main
family members referred to in the story
shown in bold.

# ACKNOWLEDGEMENTS

As usual, I am indebted to many individuals and organisations, both at home and abroad, for their valued assistance in helping to research and compile this book. My special thanks go to the Director of Culture at Sheffield City Council for the reproduction of the Spence Broughton letter, Derbyshire Records Office and Derbyshire Local Studies Library.

It would not be possible to name all the individuals who have been good enough to help and assist me during my research, but I shall make a special mention of Richard Felix and Ed Felix of Derby Gaol, Mr T. Simmons and Mrs S. Simmons of Litton, and the staff of all the various record offices and archives not only in this country but also in Australia and Tasmania. In particular, my thanks go to Mr John Taylor and Mr Clive Holliday, without whose ideas and input many of my projects would never get off the ground, and, of course, my long-suffering wife Angela.

# DEFINITIONS

**Gallows**, *gal' z, n:* a frame or apparatus usually made of wood and consisting of two vertical posts joined by one crosspiece on which convicted criminals were put to death by being hanged by the neck.

**Gibbet**, *jib'it, n:* a structure similar to a gallows, usually with a single vertical post and one protruding arm, from which the body of an executed prisoner would be exhibited after execution enclosed in chains or an iron frame as a warning to others.

# INTRODUCTION

Imagine being alone – so utterly alone, yet being surrounded by a baying crowd. No matter how you scream, beg or plead there is no hope. No hope of escape and no hope of reprieve. You are going to die and it is to be a very public death. You have been found guilty of a crime that warrants the death penalty and whether you or the crowd think it is just or not the sentence will be carried out – you *will* die, and it will be a painfully slow end as everything slows right down and time drags on for an eternity. First, you are brought from your place of confinement and into the public gaze, and as your presence becomes known an expectant silence falls, with just a few boisterous spectators calling out. Then, as the eyes of hundreds or maybe thousands of people are on you, you make your way to the scaffold and there on the raised platform, with your hands or arms bound, you are ceremoniously prepared to face your doom. Officialdom surrounds you on all sides, for justice must be seen to be done, the law must be upheld and your life has to be forfeit. As the time draws close for your demise your pulse begins to race out of control and your breathing becomes ever more rapid until, finally, it is time.

This is an imagined view indeed and has been portrayed by writers in this way for many years. The reality is much more sordid and brutal, but for centuries scenes similar to this have been played out thousands of times in all the four corners of the globe. So many men, women and children have suffered at the hands of the executioner that it is impossible to know how many have died under the title of official justice. Not all of those that died were guilty of any crime, while many of those that were guilty had only committed crimes that would today be described as minor. In England, during the period from the mid-1700s to about 1850, the number of crimes that carried the death penalty grew steadily until there were over 280. Crimes such as murder and arson carried the ultimate penalty but so did the lesser crimes of pickpocketing, cutting down a young tree, stealing goods worth five shillings (25p) and even damaging Westminster Bridge. The list was seemingly endless, but so intent were the authorities on imposing their rule that some crimes could have the alleged criminal charged twice for the same crime – albeit with slight variations in the charges – with the death penalty possibly being passed twice. It is no wonder that this draconian series of measures were to become known in later years as 'The Bloody Code'.

Such was society at the time that equality of the law was not always practised, and influence and power could have a serious outcome on the verdict. Many wealthy and influential lawbreakers failed to get as far as the courtroom simply because of the calling-in of favours or the handing out of bribes. For those that were brought to justice, found guilty and sentenced to death, they could in many cases expect a reprieve, but for those that did not, they could look forward to a date with the executioner.

The aristocracy and wealthier convicts would not be despatched in the same way as the common criminal. In France and

Germany the main method of execution for the upper classes was beheading by the sword. The prisoner would be expected to kneel with their arms down by their sides, their backs straight and their heads held high, and most importantly they were expected not to move. The executioner would then wield his specially made and extremely sharp sword in a sideways horizontal stroke and despatch the prisoner. Needless to say, in quite a lot of cases it was difficult for the prisoner to keep still simply through fear, and there are many recorded instances of them moving, with the result of ears being cut off or jaws smashed before they had to try to retake their position once again. The hardest job would fall to the executioner's assistant if the condemned was not able to remain motionless, or did not have the strength to kneel, for it was his job to hold the prisoner in the correct position. It goes without saying that it was not a part of the job that inspired confidence and it sometimes resulted in the assistant suffering from the sword as well. While the traditional methods persisted in Germany, the French eventually produced a much less haphazard method when they introduced the guillotine. Apart from being safer for the user, this method, which involved the use of a heavy, free-falling blade between two vertical uprights to despatch the prisoner pinioned beneath, also speeded up the process. Indeed, this invention was necessary to get through the sheer numbers sentenced to death during and after the French Revolution and the Reign of Terror.

In England, however, things were different. The sword and the guillotine were relatively humane methods of execution, providing the executioner knew his job, but the English method was much cruder. Despatching the noble classes followed much the same pattern in so much as the condemned had their head removed from their body. The main difference was that in England the executioner would use an axe and not a sword. In many cases this would be specially made for the purpose but not always, and sometimes it would just be a large axe that the executioner could wield with effect. Whereas the sword would cut through bone and tissue, the axe would more times than not just bludgeon its way through the vertebrae and muscle. The sword could be honed until the thin blade was razor sharp but the axe was thick and ungainly, with the result that very often the cutting edge was nearly blunt and only with brute force could it go through the prisoner's neck. Many executions were bungled by poor equipment or, even worse, poor executioners. For example, when the Duke of Monmouth was executed in 1685 for the failed rebellion against James II it took five blows of the axe to sever his head from his body. Whether this was planned or just a bungled attempt to carry out the sentence is open to dispute, but it was one of many similar events in the annals of history.

However brutal this may appear, spare a thought for those convicted of treason and who were given the full sentence as prescribed by the law. For these unfortunates they could only look forward to being hanged, drawn and quartered. They would be partly hanged until not quite dead, have their genitals cut off and burnt on a brazier in front of their eyes, their internal organs would be cut out while still alive and finally they would be beheaded and their body cut into four pieces.

Regardless of how brutal these methods were, they were nothing to those inflicted on the poor common criminal. In just about all societies, the main method of executing the commoner was by hanging. Not the speedy way, which was introduced by William Marwood in 1872 whereby the prisoner would be sent into oblivion with their neck broken after falling a calculated distance on the end of a rope (otherwise known as the 'Long Drop'), but by slow strangulation. At times, the rope would only be about 45cm (18in) long, so that the death throes could go on for as long as half an hour. The 'Short Drop', as this was called, was the preferred method in England as it was thought to be the quickest and most humane method of hanging, bringing about an almost instantaneous death. Obviously the person who thought up this method must have had a strange way of defining 'instantaneous'. If the condemned was lucky they would have a relative or friend who could pull down on his or her legs to speed up the process. Sometimes the executioner would perform the task themselves, or if the condemned could afford it then they would pay a member of the crowd to carry out the task. Seeing someone hanging onto the legs of the often wildly kicking prisoner led to the term 'hangers-on', denoting someone who is doing no good and may just be there to profit from the situation. Even after death, the body of the dead might not be released to the relatives or friends for burial but instead the judge may have ruled some other use for the body.

We must also spare a thought for the victims of crime, especially for the victims of murder. These unfortunates very often met their ends completely alone except for the murderer themselves. They could probably see the look of hate or desperation in their killer's eyes, smell their sweat and listen to their breathing, as finally they realised that death would be the only release – and, for some, a welcome release – from the excruciating pain being inflicted upon them. Some of the murders committed over the centuries have been for the strangest of reasons: some for revenge and hate; some for gain; sometimes for the most trifling of amounts. Over the following pages I shall try to instill the senselessness of many of the acts committed by human upon human in the pursuit of gain and how one family in particular and the area in which they lived seemed to bear the heavy burden of life as it slowly fell apart.

Following their defeat in the American War of Independence during the late 18th century, the British government felt as though it had enemies on all sides, not only hostile foreign powers but also individuals and groups within its own borders. Therefore, slowly but surely, it began to impose itself and its harsh rule on an unsuspecting populace. It was these increasing hardships that played a part in the terrible events that were to befall Anthony Lingard and his family in rural Derbyshire, where their story also begins during the late 18th century. This small community came to be recognised for the terrible deeds that happened around them, but it also became known for the cruel

# LOCATION OF LITTON IN BRITAIN

and harsh punishments handed out to its lawbreakers. This book will also reveal a small glimpse of the story of one boy's struggle for survival in the cotton spinning mills of the country, and in particular one mill in the village of Litton, Derbyshire. The source that tells us of this small boy's struggle are his own memories, a lone voice in a wilderness that over time has shown itself to be tragically true. By contrast, the clues to the lives of the Lingard family come from many different documents and papers, each one putting another piece of the puzzle in place.

This is the story of the tragedies and heartbreak that befell the family of Anthony Lingard and the community around him and the lasting effect they were to have on the laws of this country.

# PREPARING THE WAY

Times were hard – they always had been – and they probably always would be. That is the sort of thought that every generation has had at some time or other and more than likely will have in the future. For some, though, times really were hard and to scrape out a meagre living and to survive from one day to the next was the best that could be expected. Of course, there were the lighter moments and times of real happiness, as occasionally communities would get together to celebrate something that was to change the lives of those around them. It might be a baptism or a wedding that would unite everyone into forgetting the toils of life if only for a short period, letting them put the trials and tribulations of just existing to the back of their minds. Many years ago one such happy event happened in a place which at that time was little known outside its local area, but within a few short years would become known far and wide for the brutal and tragic events that were to occur in the surrounding countryside. How could anyone foresee that one day's happiness would lead to so much heartache and misery and would in its tragic way help to change the laws of a country and even help in the founding of a new nation. Little did Anthony Lingard realise that this chain of events would begin with his own wedding.

On 25 December 1786 Anthony Lingard of Litton in Derbyshire purposely entered the parish church of St John the

Baptist in Tideswell, a large village close to the much smaller rural hamlet from which Lingard came. As he made his way towards the altar, passing the old font in which he himself had been baptised, his eyes may just have caught sight of the carved faces that stared down from each of the stone pillars which supported the arches lining the nave or those that looked down from the wooden roof beams high above. This ancient and beautiful church, with its cold, stone flagged floor, was showing signs of neglect and its interior was in need of some repair, but standing in its somewhat aloof yet commanding position it dominated everything around. For such a remote part of the country this was indeed a magnificent place to be. Nearby would have been a number of close friends and relatives, for they were here to witness Lingard's marriage to Elizabeth Neal, a marriage that would last a lifetime through good times and bad. Coming from lowly stock, Lingard's prospects for the future were like those of the vast majority of his fellow countrymen – he was almost certainly condemned to a life of want and drudgery. No doubt today, however, his mind was on the events of the day to come, and all thoughts of tomorrow were cast aside. He would have known that this was the very same church that his parents were married in all those years ago. Such were the privations of life that Anthony Lingard's father, John, had been married twice. His first wife, Elizabeth Lingard, had died in 1755 after six years of childless marriage, but after two more years he married once again, this time to

Alice Middleton. The young Alice soon gave John a baby daughter, but fate was to deal them a taste of the future when the infant Elizabeth died from smallpox within months. In the following year, 1759, their first son was born and as tradition dictated in many families he was named after his father, so a second John entered the Lingard family. Two years later came Anthony and, finally, in 1763, William. Even now, with three sons to make up their family, John and Alice were dealt a bitter blow when at the age of 25 William died. Out of four children, two had died before their time. That is how life was and that is how it would be for many years to come. As hard and as cruel as it seems, this was normality for the men and women of the lower order, for whom harsh working conditions and poor or non-existent medical practices were part of their everyday lives. For those that weakened, fell ill or were injured, the use of a doctor or physician was a luxury that could not be afforded by the vast majority and slowly but inexorably their health would decline.

Both of John Lingard's marriages, the baptisms of his children, the burial of his first wife and of his son and daughter had taken place in the same church, the very same church that Anthony and Elizabeth were due to be married in.

Tideswell and Litton, as well as the surrounding area, are in what is now called the Peak District, a beautiful and picturesque part of the Derbyshire countryside. Lying close to Bakewell and a short distance from Sheffield, these communities are now a magnet for tourists, with the area being renowned for its rolling hills, green fields, breathtaking views and quaint villages tucked away off of the beaten track. In the 18th century things were different. Then, as now, one of the main industries was farming, but in those days this meant a hard life where nothing was predictable and the weather could ultimately decide whether there was enough to eat or not. This was not the romantic land of rolling fields of golden wheat gently waving in the breeze and orchards bursting with fruit-laden trees, but of sometimes inhospitable landscapes better suited to sheep farming, where if a harsh winter struck without all preparations being made then everybody and everything faced the prospect of starvation. In 1818 the traveller Ebenezer Rhodes described the area as '...bleak hills and plains...', and in 1857 the *Whites Directory* gave an even more depressing description when it described the area as being '...a bleak and naked land, having no hedgerows and few trees...'. It was in this type of environment that the whole community had to pull together or risk hardship and even death.

The other main source of work in the area at that time was lead mining, a hard and dangerous profession to be in, even when things were going well. The danger underground from working in those cramped and claustrophobic conditions meant that many men were killed or injured. Yet mining prospered for many years, regardless of all the risks; although little of this prosperity filtered down to the individual labourers.

Other industries more usual to the countryside still abounded but these employed fewer people. Blacksmiths, of course, were needed; all towns, cities and villages had to have a smith for the horse was 'king', and without these men horses could not be shod, and the everyday tools and repairs that a smith made meant that he was indispensable. The cordwainer, who could make shoes, was equally important, as was the cobbler, who repaired the shoes, the shopkeeper, the frame-work knitter and many more besides. All these forms of employment were around the area at that time and each and every one of them relied on their neighbours to provide them with custom. In later years, the cotton mill was to take its place as a major employer, yet here too danger was ever present as mechanisation edged its way into the everyday life of the worker. The parish registers for Tideswell show that many of the children that worked in the mills died at a young age and there are many listed in the burial records. There is no doubt at all that some of these poor children died from illness and disease, yet there can equally be no doubt that some of them died from injuries received in working in those harsh regimes. Mutilation was common among the children, for it was their task to crawl beneath the moving machinery, retrieving and joining together the broken ends of the threads. If injury or death occurred then still the machinery pounded relentlessly on: nothing short of a catastrophe ever stopped the mechanisms. Not all mill owners or managers were heartless though, and, as we shall see, one man can sometimes make a difference.

With the Industrial Revolution gathering pace, the way was open for people with vision to make their fortunes. The old ways were beginning to die out and the labour market started to be more mobile. New ideas on how businesses should be run filtered through to the new generation of entrepreneurs, who looked for ways of making a quick fortune. All over the country men were taking financial risks in the blind hope of amassing a fortune and being on a bandwagon that had no way of falling by the wayside, and yet in many cases they managed to do so. However, very often these men would enter into a venture without truly assessing the risks to their financial security or the practicality of the project. In 1782, just outside Litton in an area now known as Miller's Dale, Ellis Needham and his cousin Thomas Frith viewed the area with the idea of setting up their own business. These two men believed that they had found a way to make money in a relatively easy way. The cotton industry was rising rapidly, with all types of men throwing their cash into factories in a bid to join the elite moneyed class, and Needham and Frith hoped to be one of those at the top of the tree. On land leased from Lord Scarsdale, they sunk their money into building a new factory, which, in their eyes, was ideally situated to take advantage of natural and economic resources. Other mills soon followed in the area and this only seemed to back up the two men's belief that their investment had been a shrewd one. The faith that they had placed in their mill had, however, been misplaced and within a short time it became obvious that it was beginning to fail. Measures needed to be taken to redress the situation and just four years later it was up for sale.

With no buyer on the horizon, the partners looked for help elsewhere and turned to William Newton, who three years earlier had built a mill for Richard Arkwright at Cressbrook, just a short distance away. Perhaps this man could be the salvation for the Litton Mill venture, for although his past record was a little chequered, he did have experience and he knew his trade. Needham and Frith offered Newton a junior partnership for the princely sum of £200 on the understanding that he would repair and look after the machinery. Such was Newton's abilities that he later became partner in two more mills, yet the problems at Litton Mill continued, despite his best efforts.

The local populace was relatively sparse and even though many did leave the main industries to join the mills, the increasing number of these establishments meant that the number of workers available to employ was falling short of what was required. Coupled with this was the problem of Litton Mill's remoteness and access to it, and so even more drastic measures had to be taken to try to save the factory. With willing labour in short supply, Needham and Frith turned to parish apprentices to fill the gaps in the workforce. Children would be taken from workhouses and poorhouses and given lodgings at the factory, worked till they were exhausted, paid virtually nothing and would be fed on the worst type of food imaginable. In 1793 Needham and his partners built the first of two apprentice houses to take these children and it was perhaps at this time that Newton began to have doubts as to the moral rectitude of the venture. In the days of cruel working practices, Newton was regarded as being more lenient and kindly than many of his contemporaries. Four years after joining the partnership, he left to take over an inn that had been left to him following the death of his godmother. Years later, following the subsequent loss and regaining of his fortunes, he returned to manage Cressbrook Mill, the same mill he had built all those years before. Needham and Frith continued to persevere in their failing venture at Litton, introducing conditions and treatment of their apprentices that were becoming more and more extreme in their cruelty. Most of these apprentices were condemned to a life of hardship and danger, with no escape whatsoever because they had been indentured to the age of 21 – it was not uncommon in the mills for some of these children to be as young as five or six, occasionally even younger.

It was against this background of social upheaval that the government added greater pressures. The American War of Independence, which had been a long, hard-fought campaign, had been lost just a few short years before and in its paranoia the government began to look for revolutionaries from within its own borders as well as from abroad. For years, the British had been sinking money into foreign campaigns, money that could have been used more wisely at home, and the government was at times unstable and almost paralysed because of the illness or 'madness' of King George III. Each faction within the government and opposition dared not move too quickly or radically lest the problems with the monarchy should cause them to lose power or position. This relative inaction resulted in the government slowly but surely imposing harsher laws, and step by step it introduced conditions that meant the life for the ordinary man and woman became increasingly less hopeful and made the struggle to carry on even harder.

For the average man or woman these high-powered manoeuvrings were well above their intellectual level; their only concern was to be have enough to eat and to have a roof over their heads. It was against this background that Anthony Lingard and Elizabeth Neal took their vows on the very day that should have been a good omen – 25 December.

After the ceremony, the Lingards, as they now were, made their way back to Litton to begin their life together in the house in which Anthony Lingard probably already lived. Lingard was a farm labourer and more than likely remained that way for the rest of his life as there are several references over the years giving this as his profession. There was an ulterior motive to the wedding, however, for although time had been taken for the banns to be read in the traditional way, Elizabeth was pregnant. It is unlikely that it was an enforced marriage in the legal sense, for if it had been it is unlikely that time would have been allowed for the banns to have been read. More likely a licence would have been sought and under the duress of the parish council Lingard and Elizabeth Neal would have been brought to church by the village constables where the enforced marriage would have taken place in front of these representatives of authority. This would have been done so that the parish would have not been obliged to keep both Elizabeth and her newborn child, for it was a requirement of the law that a single mother with an illegitimate child should be kept by the parish from whence she originally came.

By June 1787 Elizabeth had given birth to her first child and on 24 June the proud parents attended the very same church in which they had married to witness the baptism of their daughter, Mary. Before the end of the following year they had been blessed with another child, this time a boy, and on 1 January 1789 baby John was also baptised in the parish church of Tideswell. As the Lingards carried on as best as they could, things were beginning to happen in the far-off reaches of Europe. How could they know that events hundreds of miles away in foreign climes would have such dire consequences in the coming years, not just for their family, but for the whole country?

When America had fought for its freedom from British rule they had been able to enlist the help of an important ally, France. As far as the British political system was concerned, the old enemy of France had been out to cause trouble and to destabilise the British economy and diminish its influence over its growing empire. In that same year the French Revolution began and the British government let out a collective sigh of relief and enthusiasm as they believed that the new regime would be weaker and mean a new French foreign policy at the very least, and at best it would be a government representing the people and would therefore relax the pressures on Britain and its populace. A respite it was indeed, albeit a temporary one. At least, it was a respite from some of the pressures from abroad for the ruling classes, whereas for the everyday person life was still hard and the relief felt by those in power failed to permeate down. All this time the government of William Pitt kept looking over its shoulder at those it suspected of subversion and in doing so was planting the seeds of despair and destitution ever more deeply.

For the next two years the Lingards made a living to feed their growing family until in 1791 a second son was born. Once again the baptism took place in Tideswell, as all the Lingard family baptisms would, and on 26 June their youngest child was proudly given his father's name of Anthony. If only they had known that Anthony Lingard the younger would in later years go down in history for perpetrating such violent deeds they might have changed the course of their lives.

That same year the screw was turned on the poorer families once again. Farmers were complaining that imports of corn were too cheap and were hitting their profits, with resultant hardships. This landed gentry class were obviously looking inwardly but the government bowed to pressure and introduced the Corn Law of 1791, which meant that the import of corn was restricted if the price fell below 50 shillings (£2.50) per quarter. The result of this was to keep the price of bread artificially high, thus making the basics of life ever more expensive. In that same year Pitt and the rest of his cabinet feared unrest and uprising following the publication of Tom Paine's *The Rights of Man* in which he supported the French example and called for democratic reform. This book sold over 200,000 copies, which was in itself remarkable considering the illiteracy of a good part of the population.

On the face of it, the common family appeared lucky to be able to survive and many of them were below the poverty line, but many were able to get by using guile and ingenuity. Britain had by this time been in the early throes of the Industrial Revolution for some time and its pace was slowly beginning to quicken so that every family was feeling its effects in some way or other. In Litton and the surrounding area the improvement in the road network was bringing some changes to everyday life. Turnpikes (or toll roads) were springing up throughout the whole of the country and Derbyshire had its fair share. Even this little backwater was crossed by turnpikes and further down the valley, just below Litton, the tiny hamlet of Wardlow Mires stood on the junction of two of these roads. It was just a relatively short walk from either Litton or Tideswell to reach Wardlow Mires either by using the toll road itself or by taking one of the unmade tracks that acted as shortcuts. The main toll road that passed through Tideswell and made its way in the direction of Baslow and Chesterfield had been there since 1759 and no doubt it had suffered its share of lawlessness. Turnpikes made their money through toll keepers, who charged travellers for using the roads which they controlled, and the toll keepers' houses were very often isolated and vulnerable. It was not for the faint-hearted to take on the job of toll keeper and many were robbed and even lost their lives to criminals who saw them an easy way to make money. They also provided the more daring with another source of income and, although not a new profession, toll roads gave the highway robber a new clientele. Highway robbery had long since passed its heyday of the late 16th and early 17th centuries, yet still it had not been eradicated. In 1722 a law was passed that imposed the death penalty for being armed and disguised on roads and heaths. The term 'disguised' could mean anything from being masked and hooded to just having the face blackened; it was a crude catch-all to put fear into any would-be robber. It need not be said that it had little effect, for the chances of being caught were far outweighed by the possibility of financial gain. The last famous highwayman to be hanged was Jerry Abershaw, who met the executioner in 1795, but by the 1830s the highwayman was a rarity, who seemed to commit the crime more out of desperation than for any true criminal intent.

For Anthony Lingard the elder and Elizabeth all these considerations and political machinations were not things to be thought about, and their only concern, as always, was for their family and themselves. Steadily, the family increased in size and in 1793 Joseph was born and in 1796 James, but by the time that James had entered into the world Britain was once again deeply embroiled in a foreign war. In 1793 France had declared war in the hope this would lead to a British Revolution on the same lines as the French. Britain was totally unprepared and diverted yet more money into the army and navy – money that was in desperate need elsewhere in the economy. The price of bread was still artificially high and the burden was heaped on as taxes were increased, until in 1799 income tax was introduced at two shillings in the pound. Incomes below £60 were exempt, however, and there were allowances for children and life insurance premiums. There is no doubt whatsoever that the Lingards did not pay income tax as this was directed primarily at the landed gentry, but there is equally no doubt that the gentry passed on the loss of income to those lower down the social scale, so for all its good intentions the tax increases were crippling already poor families like the Lingards. The year 1793 also marked the beginning of Pitt's 'Reign of Terror' whereby extreme measures were employed to suppress and eliminate all subversive people and organisations. Neighbour began to look at neighbour and wondered who could be trusted.

Less than nine months after the birth of James, their youngest child, Elizabeth and Anthony suffered a crushing blow, for in the space of 18 days they buried their sons William, Joseph and then baby James, each one a victim of an outbreak of smallpox that had struck the area. This is the first mention of William Lingard in the records, and although a baptism is mentioned for a William the son of John and Elizabeth Lingard in 1794, it seems more likely that this boy was indeed the son of Anthony and Elizabeth, who had probably been born out of the area, and that the burial records are correct. It is unlikely that the officiating clergyman, the Revd Brown, would have made such a tragic mistake and entered the incorrect details into the register. The parish records show that within days nine local children had succumbed to the illness that cut through the local tightly-knit communities, and the Lingards must have felt as though they had shouldered the brunt of it all for they had not lost one child but three. Even at a time when the child mortality rate was high, it must have come as a paralysing loss for the couple as through all their hardships the family that they loved so much had pulled through. All but two of the victims had come from the small hamlet of Litton, and for such a tiny community this high rate of attrition would only have nurtured the belief that they were to be cursed forever with pain.

While Britain had been at war, prices for food and other commodities had steadily risen, and although wages had also risen they had gone up by much less, so much so that they did not rise in real terms until about the time of the defeat of Napoleon at Waterloo in 1815. The Industrial Revolution, as already pointed out, did bring benefits: the textile industry was starting to boom, mills were springing up all over Lancashire,

Yorkshire and Derbyshire, bringing employment and lower prices for cotton goods, yet with it came disaster for the smaller manufacturer, in other words people from families such as the Lingards. These families relied on supplementing their meagre income from agriculture by working on hand looms in their own homes. Wives and children would put hours into this tedious work to make an extra income and in the evenings when the nights were long the husband would join in too. It was a case of all members of the family having to contribute to their own welfare with no exceptions.

Help was at hand for some of the labourers, however, in the form of a type of poor relief, a system called the Speenhamland System. This system, named after a village in Berkshire, was designed to help those in most need by supplementing the wages of the poorest by using money from the rates and thereby bringing their income up to a certain level. This effectively set a minimum wage, which the landowners took advantage of by either not raising their workers' wages or, in some cases, reducing them in the full knowledge that the rates would make up the shortfall. Overall, the effect was to create a class of agricultural labouring paupers and to demoralise and remove any incentive to work from the vast majority of those caught in that position. The Lingards and other families around would most probably have been caught in that terrible trap and their fears and worries can only have filtered down to their children.

# THE WORKHOUSE BOY

The privations that hit the rural areas, causing widespread poverty, had also hit the towns and cities and throughout the country the workhouses and poorhouses were filled to capacity. The elderly, infirm, destitute and orphaned arrived daily at the doors of these places of supposed sanctuary. Life inside these institutions was harsh and was led by a rigid set of regulations that saw men and women separated, with no opportunity even for married couples to communicate with each other. Life was regimented and the work the inmates were given was tedious, unskilled and left many of them with less and less hope of escaping the cycle of despair. It was regarded by many that the inmates of the workhouses were there because they were lazy and did not want to work. The thought that these unfortunates were in need of help and not punishment (although in some cases this was seen as treatment to an ailment) seemed to pass most of the officials by.

At the St Pancras Workhouse in London there were scores of children being looked after at any one time. Some of the children had been placed there by their parents, who, unable to look after them, had taken the decision to place them in the workhouse so that they had a chance of living. The remainder of the children were orphans and in 1796, the same year that James Lingard had been born, a four-year-old boy with no name was taken in a carriage by an unknown woman and left with the workhouse officials. Neither the name of this woman nor her relationship to the boy will ever be known, but as the boy grew up he became more convinced that the woman was not his mother, for he felt no sense of sadness or sorrow as she left him to his fate. While in the workhouse, the other children would have visits from well-meaning parents or relatives, yet this young boy in the whole of his stay in the institution only had one visit, and that was from a woman he did not know. Shortly after his arrival, this unknown female called to see him and when he was produced the woman gave him a penny, called him 'Saint' and said that his mother was dead. She never came again. Rumours began to spread among those in the workhouse that the boy was the product of a clergyman and his now dead mother and so he earned the nickname 'Parson', but because of his age he was more commonly called 'Young Parson'. Eventually, he would find out that he had been given the name of Robert Blincoe simply because he was said to be the son of parson Blincoe. Whether it was the truth or not, Young Parson never did find out who his parents were or where he came from.

As the days passed into weeks and the weeks into months, Blincoe would look at the outside world from the windows of the workhouse, yearning to escape through the gates of his prison into a world of excitement outside. Dark, dull and foreboding as the workhouse was, he was at least adequately fed, reasonably clothed and not overworked for his tender age.

Blincoe had no way of knowing that he was indeed fortunate to be in the situation that he found himself, for unlike many children on the outside of those prison-like gates he was at least being looked after and was not starving or searching for a bed each night. In the days before a true welfare state emerged the poor and needy relied solely on the charitable means of others to survive and if none was forthcoming then starvation was the only outcome for some. For two long years this small boy carried on with the tedium of workhouse life, until one day a rumour spread throughout the building that a party of master sweeps were to pay a visit to pick apprentices to help them in their work. Far from seeing this as a means of escape from a life of institutionalism, all of the children (except Blincoe) began to fear the visit of these men. The life of a chimney sweep's boy was hard and filled with danger, and it was not unheard-of for boys to get stuck in the chimneys they were cleaning and die while trapped. The work was hot, the air that they breathed was always full of soot and hot embers would burn their skin. Far from being a way of making a reasonable living and learning a skill, it was seen as a life-shortening experience that only just fell short of a living death. As the appointed day for the master sweeps' visit came, tension and fear built up inside all those expected to parade for these men, yet Blincoe could not understand this apprehension. To him, this was a chance to get out into the big wide world, a chance to be someone other than a workhouse orphan, and more importantly he saw it as a way to be free of the shackles of a regulated institution. He laughed and ran around in excitement as the anticipation of leaving his prison built up. For a six-year-old he knew he was small but when the time came to take his place in the line up of proposed apprentices he made himself as big as he could and he did his best to make himself noticeable. One by one the master sweeps walked up and down the line, and one by one they chose their apprentices, but each time they came to Blincoe they passed him by because of his small stature and appearance. At the end of the day all of the children were filled with dismay and apprehension, even Blincoe; his friends because they were doomed to a fate of dirt and ill-health and Blincoe because he had failed to be chosen. Once again he felt alone, unwanted and trapped. Life returned to the same as before, one of drudgery, toil and sorrow.

Human emotion can overcome many obstacles and Anthony Lingard the elder and Elizabeth must have been made of stern stuff for in 1798 Elizabeth gave birth once again, calling their new son James. It was common practice to reuse the name of a deceased child on a subsequent newborn, and so the tradition was continued. The following year Martha was born but sadly only lived for a short while. So far the Lingards had produced eight children, of which four had died – a 50 per cent mortality rate – and the consequences must have had a profound effect on both parents. By this time young Anthony Lingard would have been about nine years old and in his short life would have witnessed the falling standards of living within his family home and the death of three of his siblings – who knows what was going through his mind by this time? Conditions were to get harder for all those in the household over the next 10 years or so, however, as the number of children within the family increased dramatically. Between 1800 and 1809 a further six children were born: Hannah, a second Martha, another William (who, along with his elder brother Anthony, would grow up in later years to be talked about in hushed tones because of his wicked deeds), Elizabeth, Samuel and, finally, Alice. In a little over 22 years Anthony Lingard the elder and his wife Elizabeth had brought 14 children into the world, of which four had been taken away from them through death, and all throughout this period their standard of living could not have been at all high. It would be more truthful to say that it was probably a day-to-day struggle that made it a necessity for all able-bodied members of the family to work, and work they would, regardless of age or sex. Respite did come at one point when Britain was for a short period at peace with its neighbours and in 1810–11 a small economic boom took place, but this was only temporary and poverty and depression soon set in again.

There are no records at all to show that any of the Lingard family did anything to break the law of the land, yet it is hard to believe that everything they ate or possessed was obtained by pure legal methods. It is quite likely that poaching and other such activities took place; it was very common in the countryside but was dependant on the poacher not being caught. Punishment if found out was harsh indeed and would more than likely lead to the death penalty or a period of transportation to some foreign land. Following the introduction of the Black Act by Parliament in 1723, the death penalty was freely administered for all kinds of crimes with over 250 offences ending in the perpetrator being executed. With the war with France in full force, more and more draconian measures were introduced. It was a capital offence to burn haystacks, for example, because of the rising price of corn, which had continued relentlessly on. The government needed to make sure the country could produce as much food as possible and the landed class resented the lower class reducing their profits. There had been a spate of such incidents as frustrations were taken out against the property of such landowners and it was perceived (in many cases correctly) that while the labouring class starved, the landed farmers lined their pockets with the profits of high-priced produce.

It had been the case up until the American War of Independence that most of Britain's criminals were either given some form of corporal punishment, were transported to America or given the ultimate penalty of death; virtually none of those convicted spent long periods behind bars on land. After Britain lost the war, prisoners were sent onto hulk ships, which were usually dismasted, rotting ships that were pressed into service to act as floating gaols simply because the county gaols and other such buildings were not designed for long-term incarceration for large numbers of prisoners. By the late 1780s a solution had been found and nearly all the prisoners found guilty of serious offences where capital offences had been committed or offences that deemed a long-term prison sentence were transported on prison ships to the far-off country of Australia. Some of the unfortunates ended up in Gibraltar and some in the West Indies, but these were few in number compared to those sent to the other side of the world.

Yet still the country faced unrest and in 1811 the Luddites, a group of rioters led by someone allegedly called Ned Ludd and who was supposedly living in Sherwood Forest, set about smashing up to a thousand stocking frames that they claimed were making low-quality goods. It is very doubtful that Ned Ludd even existed but it is a fact that these machines were destroyed by the very people who they were putting out of work as mass production was once again taking away the living of the labouring classes. As a result of all these factors, the government began to use agents to infiltrate organisations that it regarded as illegal and frequently used *agent provocateurs* to stir up trouble so that it could pre-empt any actions it did not care for.

While all these social changes were taking place, the life of Robert Blincoe dragged on mercilessly in the St Pancras Workhouse. Once the immediate affect of the visit by the master sweeps had passed, a calmness entered into the lives of all the inmates until the following year, when another rumour swept among those left inside. This time it was said that the overseers and churchwardens of St Pancras had come to an agreement with the owner of a large cotton mill near Nottingham to send some of the children to work there as apprentices. They would work there till the age of 21, during which time they would be taught a trade. Once they had finished their apprenticeships they would be free to travel wherever they wanted and earn as much as they could. Once again, the by now seven-year-old Blincoe became overcome by eagerness and excitement at the prospect of escape and the chance of seeing the outside world from a different perspective. As the day of the cotton master's viewing came closer, it became apparent that so many children would be needed in the mill that the majority of those in the workhouse would be accepted for the trip to north, and this only increased the general anticipation. The day before the arrival of the cotton master it was made common knowledge among the children that those who chose to make the trip to Nottingham were to have a life beyond belief. Each of the boys and girls were to undergo such a transformation that they would soon be changed into ladies and gentlemen, they would have money in their pockets, be given silver watches and be allowed to ride their masters' horses. Yet the promises did not end there, for it was also said that they would dine on roast beef and plum pudding and they could work as they wished. Should they wish to they could rest, and work was to be something that they would decide to take part in if they wanted to. Any doubts that they had as to the validity of these promises were easily swept aside since the origin of these stories was none other than parish officers themselves and not the nurses or workhouse staff. With these stories ringing in their ears, the children's eagerness for a new life grew and grew. Little did they realise that all of these stories were lies. It was common practice in the workhouses to tell stories such as this to the pauper children so that they would go to their new masters voluntarily as they could not be forced or compelled to go if they did not wish to.

The cotton master's arrival saw the children paraded for inspection. Their health, willingness and eagerness to leave were examined and all those deemed to be seven years or over who appeared suitable were accepted. Eighty boys and girls were chosen to make their way to Messrs Lambert's mill at Lowdham near Nottingham, which meant that the St Pancras Workhouse would be almost devoid of children (for a short while at least).

The chance of finally escaping his prison surroundings made Blincoe's imagination run wild at the prospect of a new life. He found he could not sleep, his appetite fell away and his whole attitude became one of arrogance. He was not alone in his personality change, for all of his friends that had been chosen along with him went through this change as well. After all, were they not to become ladies and gentlemen? Surely this would place them in a high-ranking position on the social ladder?

Finally, the day of departure came around and eagerly this huge number of pauper children loaded into the two large wagons that would take them on their long trip north. Even at this late hour the officers of St Pancras perpetuated the myth that these unfortunates were on their way to a better life. Each of the children had been given two new suits of clothing, one for work and one for best, a new handkerchief, a shilling in cash and a large piece of gingerbread, all of which only helped to reinforce the belief that they were on their way to a better life. Accompanied by a small number of adults, they started off on their long trip to Lowdham Mill and the babble of expectation soon fell away. The journey to Nottinghamshire took four days to complete over the sometimes rough and rugged roads. The wagons lurched in every rut and hole and by the time the party of apprentices had arrived at one of their new masters' warehouses in Nottingham they were exhausted and many of them wished to go back to London. Without being given the opportunity to show regret, they were rushed into one of the buildings and there fed upon the most basic of foods – no plum pudding and no roast beef – and no talk of riding their masters' horses or any of the other promises.

The next day, now that they were somewhat refreshed, Blincoe and his friends were taken to Lowdham Mill and saw for the first time the place that was to be their home until they reached the age of 21. Much to their distress, the apprentice house bore many of the characteristics of the St Pancras

Workhouse – large, overbearing and unfriendly. As soon as the wagons stopped, they were quickly shown into a very large room furnished with tables and benches, and all around them hung the disgusting smell of oils and other noxious substances. A supper of milk porridge (which looked blue) and rye bread (a bread that was usually darker and heavier than bread made with wheat) was given to them and yet, hungry as they were, they could not eat it. To relieve the tension, the children began to throw the meagre portions of bread around until the governor in charge of them brought down his whip on the table with such force it made them all jump in fear. He had not uttered one word and discipline had been restored, such was the overbearing personality of this man. In an instant he had gone and from elsewhere in the factory a noise arose that grew louder until at last the doors of the large dining hall burst open and in rushed the apprentices who were already working in the mill. Blincoe watched in disbelief as the band of poorly dressed boys and girls dashed to the serving hatch to receive just a few boiled potatoes. Having quickly devoured their meagre rations, some of them ran across to the newly arrived apprentices and greedily finished off any porridge or bread that had been left. Not only were these children dressed in the most basic of clothing, with some of them not having jackets, caps or even shoes, every one of them was filthy with oil and grime and emitting a foul smell from lack of washing and the all-pervading malodorous oils. Although they were instructed to wash morning and night, they had never been issued with soap and weariness would overtake them before basic personal hygiene could be performed. Knives, forks and plates were not used simply because they were not issued and they pushed all their food into their mouths using unwashed, stinking hands. No sooner had this meal been hastily downed when a bell rang and off shot this ragtag collection of boys and girls, making their way quickly to the dormitories and bed. As the older apprentices made their way out, the fearsome governor returned to take the new boys to their beds, while the governor's wife took the girls to theirs. In the dormitory the apprentices slept two to a bed and Blincoe was billeted with one of the older boys, but try as he might he could not sleep. The disbelief in his situation and the overpowering smell of oils that was coming from his fellow bed mate and all those around him meant that his mind would not settle. Surely, Blincoe thought to himself, the overseers of the St Pancras Workhouse had been misled by his new masters and if they knew the truth they would rescue him and his friends. It would be many years before he came to realise the awful truth.

Blincoe did finally manage to snatch a small amount of sleep when weariness overtook him just before it was time to be up. At a little before five in the morning, he was roused as his bedfellow jumped out of bed at the sound of a bell, the boy telling Blincoe to get dressed quickly or he would get a beating and miss breakfast. Before he could comply with these instructions in walked the governor with his whip and, rounding up the new boys, he herded them downstairs for their black bread and porridge. The new boys were slower than the older ones in getting ready and so were the last to get anything to eat. Once again they found the food hard to stomach and once again if any food was left it was swiftly snatched up by the older apprentices. By half past five they had completed their repulsive meal and had been taken to the mill to be set to work.

When Blincoe entered the mill it was already in full production and he was astounded at the intense noise that filled the air and the horrible stench that filled his nostrils. These mechanised mills were filled with vast rows of noisy machinery that covered most of the floor space; every square inch was utilised for the making of money. The Spinning Mule, the Spinning Jenny or Arkwright's Water Frame were the favoured types of equipment, taking up to 80 spindles of yarn each. These cumbersome machines with their exotic names were potential death traps and little thought was given towards the health and safety of the operators. Its low ground clearance, along with the myriad of twisting yarns and bobbins, made it difficult for men to get access if the yarns broke or became snagged and that is why so many children and women were employed in mills. They were believed to be small and nimble enough to be able to dodge in and out of the working parts as the factory was kept at full production. Each one of these machines had a vast array of fast-moving parts that were exposed to the elements, with no protective guards covering the dangerous equipment. Amid the confusing clamour of pounding machinery, Blincoe was given his first task of picking up all the loose cotton. To start with he thought that this was an easy job to perform but slowly the constant bending over gave him backache, the incessant noise from the never-ending machinery and the terrible smell soon made him feel ill, and all the time he went about his duties he was not allowed to sit or rest. Not until 12 o'clock, after a full six and a half hours of non-stop work, was he allowed any respite, when mercifully the bell rang to herald dinner. All the apprentices ran out of the factory, with Blincoe gratefully among them, eager to get into the fresh air and to get whatever food was on offer, and it would never in all his days there be roast beef and plum pudding.

For the next week or so Blincoe was kept at this back-breaking task and along with all the other workers in the mill he breathed deeply on the fetid and dust-laden air within, until he was given a kind of promotion when he was made a roving winder. His tender years meant that he was too short to do his job properly, so he was given something to stand on, and when he found he could not keep up with the swiftly moving machinery he was beaten. The beatings became such a normal part of his everyday life that he was covered in bruises on most of his body and it was usual to have his hair pulled, to be kicked and sworn at. If for any reason production was lost then the workers had to stop behind to make up for the loss, and it was not at all strange for them to work 14 hours a day, six days a week, with Sundays outwardly left for rest. The conditions suffered by this seven-year-old boy affected both his physical and mental health and so, determined to let the overseers at St Pancras know the conditions in which he and his fellow apprentices were being kept in, he decided to escape and make his way to London. Taking stock of the situation, he managed to sneak out one day and headed towards Burton, a nearby town, with the intention of catching a lift to London and thus to St Pancras Workhouse, but luck was not on his side. While Blincoe walked down the main street of Burton he was seen by a local tailor, who invited the boy into his premises. Once inside, he plied the boy with food so that he would be more relaxed, calm and unable to flee. It was then that the tailor let it be known that he recognised Blincoe from the mill at Lowdham and that he was going to take the young boy back. Donning his outdoor clothes, the tailor took the young boy and began to walk him back to Lowdham, where he returned this unwilling boy to the same place from whence he had just come and, as was the custom, received the five shillings he was entitled to for his efforts. So many children tried to escape the bondage of mill apprenticeships all over the country that it was common practice for rewards to be offered for the return of these wayward strays, and in some cases it provided a lucrative if irregular income to some enterprising individuals. The conditions in the mills and the working practices employed by the mill owners was for the most part unknown to the public at large but here and there budding entrepreneurs found that it was possible to turn even the trade in children's lives to their advantage.

Once the tailor had left, Blincoe was beaten as never before and then sent back to work, his spirit almost broken. Time and again he had seen his friends injured while working around the flying machinery until finally it was Blincoe's turn to suffer excruciating pain when part of a finger was torn off after being caught in some moving parts. With blood pouring from the open wound, he was taken to the local surgeon, patched up and sent back to work at the mill. None of his workmates offered any sympathy, for this type of accident was all too common and did not rate a second glance, some gave sarcastic jibes but that was all.

Life in the unrelenting mill went on and beatings, lack of sleep and near starvation rations became part of the everyday grind. Weeks became months and months became years and it was during his second year at Lowdham that Blincoe witnessed an accident of horrific proportions. Mary Richards, a pretty girl of about 10 years of age, was working at a drawing frame late one night. Most of the others had gone from work and the mill was becoming empty. As Mary was taking off the weights from the machine her dress caught in the driveshaft that ran below it. Amid screams of pain, Mary was dragged into the machine as the driveshaft pulled her in and began to throw her wildly round. As she flailed around, Blincoe watched in despair as her arms, legs, thighs and many other bones were broken, the sound of each snap reaching his ears above the noise of the machinery. The floor and the machinery were sprayed with Mary's blood and all the time she was screaming until, finally, everything stopped. The driveshaft ceased in its motion simply because Mary's broken body had jammed the workings – and she was still alive. Carefully her body was extricated and she was taken to the physician, yet by some miracle she survived and very slowly began to recover. She eventually returned to work as a broken cripple – one more victim of the relentless quest for profit.

The following year a committee was sent by the overseers of St Pancras Workhouse to examine conditions at Lowdham Mill after they had received a complaint by the mother of two sisters who worked there. These two young girls had smuggled out a letter to their mother telling her of the conditions they worked under and imploring her to help. After making her own enquiries, the mother took all the necessary steps to save her children and contacted the authorities, insisting that they should act. The committee laid down a series of rules and conditions for the mill to adhere to but, perhaps because of these rules or possibly the state of the economy at that time, the mill soon closed its doors for good. All the apprentices that could find work elsewhere were allowed to go and those that could contact parents or relatives to take them in were also allowed to leave. Blincoe had neither relatives nor another apprenticeship to go to so he and the remainder were sold on to another mill owner, for whom they would finish off the indenture. They thought that they had survived a hell on earth but little did they realise the mill they were going to would make Lowdham seen like a paradise. They had been sold to Ellis Needham of Litton Mill.

# LITTON MILL

B y 1802 Anthony Lingard Snr and his wife Elizabeth were still eking out a living in the sometimes desolate lands around Litton. The fine weather of the summers allowed a pleasant interlude between the hard winters that prevailed in this part of the country and made their lives a little less burdensome. In their home, conditions would have been cramped and overcrowded, for by now they had six surviving children to care for and during the latter part of the year Elizabeth found she was once again pregnant. All of their children would have worked to help boost the family coffers. The young four-year-old James would have been given the simplest of tasks to help his mother, who was nursing his younger sister Martha at the time. It was normal for the family as a whole to sit down after dark and do the everyday tasks of mending clothes or possibly even weaving cloth on a frame set in the corner. It would be the task of the younger children to card or twist the wool, ready for their parents or older siblings to take and weave it into usable lengths. From repairing work tools to making simple horn lamps, all these tasks were done after the sun had set, for daylight was too valuable a commodity to be wasted. If it was at all possible, every minute of natural light had to used in the pursuit of providing food for all the members of the family, and for some families this would include caring and providing for elderly and infirm parents. Should any

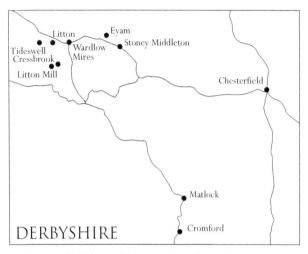

of the household be unable to do their share of manual labour or work in the fields due to infirmity they would help inside the home by taking up the duties of the younger children. Anthony Lingard the younger was by now 11 years old and his duties were completely different from those of the younger members of his family. He and the older children would help their father in his work duties or try to make an income by finding employment elsewhere and enhance the family fortunes in this way. None of the Lingard children would receive any formal education at all. Reading and writing were skills that they did not have the time for or the chance to learn. It was work that would keep them fed, and who would teach them these skills anyway?

In the towns and cities the prospects for children of the lower order were generally grim, with a future of living in the squalid conditions of cramped houses, poor sanitation and incurable diseases. The increasing mechanisation of once cottage industries was drawing more and more people into urban life and the threat of dysentery, tuberculosis and many other potentially fatal illnesses did little to stem this flow as the old way of life disappeared. By contrast, the child who lived in the country could suffer from hardships of a different kind. Hard work and illness were just as much a threat here but add to this the chance of starvation from crop failure and the possibility of dying from cold as a harsh winter set in. Although disease was ever present in the countryside, the lack of serious overcrowding of neighbourhoods meant that it was less of a problem.

Whether they realised it or not, the Lingards were rubbing shoulders with two ways of life; they with their country ways while just a short distance away was the industrialisation of Litton Mill. In November of that year, as the Lingards went about their everyday duties, Robert Blincoe and his fellow apprentices were making their way to the mill at Litton aboard carts. This long journey had taken two days to complete and they had stopped in Cromford for an overnight break. It was towards the end of the second day that they arrived at their destination. The mill here was described as being '…at the bottom of a sequestered glen and surrounded by rugged rocks, remote from any human habitation…'

Upon arrival, the apprentices were taken through the mill to their new lodgings and were able to see the conditions in which they were to work and to also see their future workmates. All of them were utterly dismayed to see the ragged condition of the other apprentices: their clothes were even more dirty, torn and dishevelled than those worn by the apprentices from Lowdham and their physical appearance was one of extreme weakness and poor health. As at Lowdham, the mill reeked with vile smells that hung heavy in the air. Ventilation had to be kept to a bare minimum in this type of establishment so that the humidity levels could be kept high, which allowed the materials to remain workable. Every available bit of floor space was taken up with a vast array of pounding, eardrum-shattering machinery. Litton Mill's favoured type of textile machinery was the Water Frame, which was a huge financial investment and one of the most efficient of its type, yet it was still a lethal weapon if it was not given full respect. In the apprentices' lodgings Blincoe and his comrades were given a meal of porridge made from water and oat cakes, which was so unpalatable that many did not take their food. If the food at Lowdham had been regarded with disdain, they saw this present offering as unfit for even the lowest of beasts.

The beds that they were to sleep in were also of an inferior nature to those at Lowdham and many, including Blincoe, found they could not sleep that night. His mind in turmoil, this young boy contemplated just how bad things had become. Their previous place of employment had been seen as a place of cruelty, a living hell, but in comparison to their new abode it was a heaven. The bell that tolled to rouse them from their beds and so to work sounded at four o'clock in the morning, not five as before, and was yet another sign of the privations to come.

On his first day at work Blincoe noticed the appalling injuries that his new workmates were carrying. Each of them was covered in cuts and bruises and many of them had injuries to the head that were infested and crawling with 'vermin'. Personal washing was not performed because there was no soap and no one had the time or energy to perform the task. The apprentices themselves could almost be described as walking slums: weak, sickly, dirty and perpetually tired. Breakfast came at around eight o'clock after nearly four hours of continual toil, yet it was normal for it to finally arrive two or three hours late. It consisted of the most inedible foods possible, yet if they did not eat it they would starve. Over time, the poor quality and lack of food coupled with excessive working led Blincoe and many of the others to faint or collapse while at their work, leading to the inevitable beatings. When, after a long day's work, the apprentices were allowed back to their accommodation it was to find that the evening meal was another round of repulsive fare and that sleep was to be taken in a room that housed up to 50 tired and worn-out workers. The all-pervading smell of unwashed bodies and dirty, oily clothes soon became an accepted part of life and slowly began to be unnoticed.

The poor diet that was fed to the workers and apprentices at Litton Mill was in some part mirrored in mills all around the country. Here and there more humane masters would treat their charges with respect and humanity, with the majority of masters doing just enough to satisfy public perception. Litton Mill, under the leadership of Ellis Needham, however, stood out for the extreme and excessive treatment that was endured by its apprentices. Such was the poor state of health in the mill that it was not uncommon for sickness and disease to break out. In one outbreak Blincoe estimated that out of a total of about 160 apprentices no less than 40 were struck down in one bout of fever. 'Factory fever', which was similar to 'gaol fever' (later renamed typhus), was ever present and hung in the background, waiting for the right conditions to explode among the weak and vulnerable. At Litton the doctor's remedy of less work and better food was only administered in part and once things had abated the usual routine returned. In a lot of the cases of sickness, death was something that was accepted and in some respects expected because life in a mill was cheap. If one of the apprentices fell ill at their machines they would not be allowed to take to their bed and would have to continue at their post until they passed out or worse. It was only then that they would be taken to the dormitory and left to their own devices. Medical care was of such a basic sort that it would be fair to say it virtually did not exist at all.

Illness and disease was just one thing that the apprentices had to endure on an occasional basis; the real threat to their physical well-being and health was the constant beatings they received. All the overlookers and masters would beat the apprentices on a daily basis, with Blincoe being particularly singled out by one man called Robert Woodward. This particular overseer took great pleasure in handing out various forms of intricate and acute torture to him. He would kick Blincoe with such ferocity that the force would lift the child off the floor and he hit him with his hands so hard it would knock him to the floor. Should this form of punishment become boring or tedious, Woodward would vary his pleasure by using implements as a form of torture and he would pick up a rope, a stick or a leather belt with its iron buckle prominent and flail the desired implement at the young man. Along with the other overlookers in the mill, Woodward often used to throw rollers at the apprentices one after another, purposefully aiming for the unprotected heads of these unfortunates with the intention of causing serious injury and very often knocking the victim senseless and inflicting wounds that poured with blood. This cruel treatment was carried out so often that Blincoe's wounds never had time to heal before the next round of torture was inflicted and his body was never free from pain or lesions. When the head wounds of the apprentices became infected and filled with parasites a doctor would be called in, who would apply a 'pitch cap' to the head. When the covering of pitch or tar had set and was completely stuck to the head the doctor would lift one corner of the cap and, using it as a lever, would rip the cap off in one swift movement, leaving the victim in total agony.

Nor did the agony end there, for Woodward and his cohorts had designed even greater methods of inflicting pain on Blincoe and the others. On many occasions Blincoe had his hands tied together over a cross beam that ran above the machine that he was operating and, so as to save his feet and ankles from injury, he had to lift up his legs each time the mechanism went in and out. Failure to do so would ensure he got another beating, and only when his strength had failed him was he cut down so that in his weaken state he could start work again and receive more beatings for inefficiency. During the winter months he would be stripped to the waist and have heavy weights hung from his shoulders, again causing great pain. If the overlookers were in a particularly sadistic mood they would file the teeth of the apprentices, with the excuse that it would make it easier for them to eat their food. The list of tortures that was endured in Litton Mill grew with time and later included the piercing of ears, which only added to the apprentices' misery. The overlookers grew their fingernails so that they could grip the ear of one of these unfortunates and then squeeze with their fingertips until their nails passed through the flesh of the ear and met, causing extreme pain in the victim and, of course, ensuring a large flow of blood. Amid all this stood Ellis Needham, the mill owner, and far from halting these practises he at times took part. Not only did he participate in the beatings that took place, but it was also one of his favoured practices to join in with the piercing of the apprentices' ears using his own fingernails.

So desperate were some of the apprentices that they would try to escape, and on one occasion one of the boys tried to escape from an upper floor of the apprentices' house at night. He tied together some blankets and started to climb down the makeshift ladder, only to fall on to the solid ground below when one of the knots slipped. The boy later died of his injuries.

One of the apprentices that had come from the St Pancras Workhouse with Blincoe suffered beatings to such an extent that he suffered from a form of madness, which made him incapable of work and unable to feed himself. When Blincoe plucked up the courage to complain about his friend's treatment he himself had his food withheld, and when winter arrived he was stripped off and towed around the waters of the mill dam by a rope under his arms. At the point when insensibility started to overcome him, he was placed under a pump and while cold water was poured over his head, another of his tormentors threw buckets of water at his body.

Over and over again this vast array of tortures was inflicted on the apprentices, yet throughout this the machinery in the mill pounded relentlessly on, making Ellis Needham a rich man. Month after month, year after year, this regime continued, with no help for those on the inside coming from those on the outside. In 1802, the same year in which the apprentices arrived from Lowdham, Parliament had passed the first-ever Factory Act when the Health and Morals of Apprentices Act was passed. Its promoter, Sir Robert Peel, father of the later famous statesman, hoped to improve the lives of all types of apprentices; although it was primarily directed at those in cotton and woollen mills. The main provisions were that the working hours must not exceed 12 hours and the working day must start no sooner than six in the morning and end no later than nine at night, with Sundays left free for religious instruction. For the first four years of their apprenticeships, they were to be schooled every day in reading and writing, the workplace was to be well ventilated and they were to receive at least two suits with shoes and stockings. With this battery of legislation in place, the mills of Great Britain should have been a safer place to work, but with no one to enforce or police the new regulations, factory and mill owners found they had nothing to fear and so things carried on as before, with those inside either ignorant of the law or not able to see them enforced. In many cases, the officials charged with upholding the law were either the friends of the factory owners or else received a well placed sum of money which would secure a lack of interest in a particular site.

The average working day for the Litton apprentices has been estimated at 16 hours and the beatings were so regular that very often they did not know the reason for most of them. It was on one of these occasions that Blincoe was taken to Ellis Needham's son for punishment. Blincoe was ordered to strip so that the thrashing could be performed but when young Needham saw the condition of his already battered back Blincoe was sent away, for Needham feared that to inflict more injury would end in Blincoe's death.

To try to supplement their rations of food, the mill workers would steal the food given to the pigs that were on site (the pigs were for the consumption of the master and his family and not for the benefit of the apprentices), until their ruse was discovered and the pigs were more closely guarded. They would also eat the 'meal' that they were given, which was supposed to be used as a soap, and it was a treat to be able to retrieve some food scraps from the dung heap.

A blacksmith called William Palfrey, who worked at the mill and lived in nearby Litton, could hear the noise of the machinery and the cries of the apprentices as they were beaten while he worked in his room below, and this man showed sympathy towards them by buying them some food with their hard earned pennies. The apprentices were allowed to earn extra money if they agreed to work during their dinner hours, with their rate of pay for forfeiting their rest usually varying between one farthing and one halfpenny. In practice this was seldom paid by the masters, who would make the unfortunate apprentice wait until a certain amount had accrued and would then only pay part of the sum owed. Occasionally, the masters did pay and in the case of those at Litton the happy recipients of this money would secretly contact the blacksmith and ask him to purchase food on their behalf. When the overlookers were distracted or working elsewhere, the young workers would sneak downstairs to Palfrey and take possession of this veritable feast, which sometimes amounted to just a fish and a wheat cake. Blincoe once had enough money to spend sixpence (2.5p) on buying food, but his stomach was so used to the poor food served by the mill that his extravagance made him feel ill and he could not face any food the following day.

If the masters believed that an apprentice was likely to run away the poor unfortunate would be taken to the blacksmith, who would then be obliged to fix irons and fetters on them so that flight was nigh-on impossible and obedience would be almost guaranteed. Both sexes suffered the indignity of having irons fastened to their ankles and waist, with chains taking up the distance between them and thus giving them the appearance of convicts. The chains were kept on for 24 hours a day, which meant that eating, sleeping, work and toilet activities had to be performed as best as possible, and if this meant that work slowed down they would receive a beating as well.

The harsh and severe treatment that was meted out to both sexes led to many mental and emotional problems. Depression and anxiety was an everyday state of mind that many found too hard to manage. A young woman named as Phebe Rag *(sic)* found herself at such a low point that she made her way to the mill dam, took off her shoes and jumped in. One person who happened to be walking past saw her shoes and, out of curiosity, stopped. At that moment the young woman surfaced from beneath the water and the quick-thinking man leaned out and grabbed her by her hair. She was narrowly rescued from a watery death and it was to be her good fortune that this act of desperation turned out to be her ticket to freedom. When Ellis Needham heard about the incident he ordered that she be taken home and was thus freed from the mill. This was not the action of a kindly man, who was caring for his fellow creature, but of a selfish mill owner, who feared that the choice of suicide would become a popular way out of the servitude that was his by right.

The years slowly rolled by and finally Blincoe's time as an apprentice was drawing towards its conclusion. During his time at the mills his indenture had meant that he was in servitude to his masters as a virtual slave, firstly to the Lambert brothers at Lowdham Mill and latterly to Ellis Needham at Litton. In return, he should have received schooling in a trade or profession that would serve him as a useful skill and would carry him through life. As it turned out he and all the apprentices had been used purely as cheap labour with no thought or effort going into any form of schooling, whether it be for academic or practical skills. With his growing maturity, Blincoe's understanding of his future prospects began to come together. Far from being a free spirit that could travel the world outside, he realised that he would be tied to a limited circle of employers and would only be able to undertake some of the lower-paid jobs. With this realisation came a growing sense of independence and a belief that he had a right to rule his own destiny. He was still beaten and suffering the indignity of incessant punishments on a regular basis, but now he was changing into a grown adult and thoughts of rebellion entered his mind.

One day Blincoe and three of his friends, William Haley, Thomas Gulley and John Emery, deciding that they should not be so overworked, made an agreement to leave the factory at the end of a normal shift and to work no more that day. After 14 hours at work the four friends downed tools and made their way back to the apprentices' house to rest. Word was sent to Ellis Needham, who was so incensed at their actions that in his fury he ordered that they all be turned out of their accommodation. Blincoe managed to find assistance from one of his friends, who put him up for the night, while his fellow conspirators slept outside in the woods. The following morning they all returned to the mill to be taken before Needham.

The mill owner was in such a state of fury that he tore off Blincoe's waistcoat and jacket and laid into him with his walking stick. The blows rained down so heavily that the stick broke and as soon as he could Blincoe made his escape, leaving his friends to share a similar fate to the one he had endured. With this beating Needham perhaps thought he had restored order to a situation that could have set a bad example to the other workers, for if this small group of men could get away with only working 14 hours in a day what would the rest of the mill workers do?

Needham had completely misjudged the situation, however, for Blincoe had no intention of letting his humiliation over the years go unpunished. After returning to work for the morning like all the others, he broke at midday for his meal. Eating it as quickly as possible, he then set off out of the mill towards the dwelling of a local magistrate, a full 11 miles from Litton. When he finally arrived he was dismayed that the magistrate's servant would not let him in and instead directed Blincoe to return the following day to see the judge as he presided over his official duties at the Bulls Head in Eyam. In those days, minor court cases and other types of official duties, such as inquests, that took place out of urbanised areas, would be held in public buildings like inns or ale houses. This was done primarily as a matter of practicality because of travelling difficulties and because the ale houses were also well-known locations, easily found by anyone wishing to attend.

Wearily and dejectedly, Blincoe made his way back to Litton Mill, arriving back late that evening where he was immediately set to work. The irate works manager interrogated Blincoe as to his absence that day and upon being told about the trip to see the magistrate he almost exploded with threats and promises. The next day Blincoe returned to work for a short while and then, stealing himself for more retribution, he crept out of the mill and once again made his way to see the magistrate.

Arriving at the Bulls Head, he immediately made himself known to the clerk of one of the magistrates and began to recall his tale of pain and misery as the clerk busily wrote down the pitiful story. Blincoe was then taken before the magistrates and closely questioned. When it was all done one of the magistrates ordered Blincoe to return to the mill to await developments, but so alarmed was he at the prospects of receiving another beating that at first he refused. It was not until he was given a letter to be handed to John Needham, the son of Ellis, that he agreed to go back, for he was given the impression that the letter would provide him a form of protection.

Upon returning to the mill, Blincoe gave the letter to the manager, explaining once again where he had been and why. With violent protestations ringing in his ears, he returned to his usual routine. The next day the letter was handed to John Needham and just like his father he went into a fit of rage and called for Blincoe to be brought to him. With the wayward apprentice in front of him, John Needham ordered him to strip and began to thrash him with a whip, using as much force as he could muster. Blincoe's cries for him to stop went unheeded and with Needham continually swearing and cursing as he mercilessly flogged the young man, the punishment went on and on until the master's fury was vented and he began to tire from the effort. His anger satiated, he ordered the apprentice to put his shirt on and sent him back to work.

The beating did not have its desired effect, however, and once more Blincoe was determined to see justice prevail so that the world could see the true reality of mill life for an apprentice. He waited until the following Sunday night and once again furtively crept out of the mill, mindful that no one should see him. In towns and cities street lighting was in its infancy – London had experimented with the idea in 1807 when a stretch of Pall Mall had artificial lighting installed – so in the wilds of Derbyshire it was easy in the dark of night to just disappear into the rolling countryside. In his mind he determined to see the magistrate yet again and to pursue his quest for justice. After resting the night in the house of a friend, who also worked at the mill, Blincoe set off to see the magistrate. After a very long, tiring walk he reached his destination and to his dismay the magistrate despatched him to his clerk some miles off. Reluctant to go, he explained to the magistrate that the clerk and his master were almost partners in crime because of their close association, so, to alleviate his fears, the magistrate wrote a letter, which he was to hand across to the court official. Making his way to the clerk's house, he was invited into the kitchen to wait. All day he sat there until he realised that the clerk would never see him or read the letter on which he pinned so much hope. Reluctantly, he gave up and made his way back to the mill to take his punishment once more. When he arrived back he again explained where he had been and why, only this time he was so despondent he pleaded that if he were not beaten as before he promised that he would not repeat his escapades. Blincoe was never beaten again. So many boys and girls died in Litton Mill that Ellis Needham and his son John had these poor unfortunates buried in different parishes so that the alarm would not be raised and their working practices investigated.

In 1813 Blincoe reached the age of 21 and became free of his indenture after nearly 11 years in one of the hardest regimes imaginable. Yet, compared to some of the other apprentices that had come with him from St Pancras Workhouse and latterly Lowdham Mill, he had fared quite well. He had not received the most severe beatings nor the most punishment, yet his story so far was nevertheless one of pain and endurance. Now that he was free, though, what of the future?

As the events in Litton Mill had unfolded over the years, life in Litton village had progressed. The stories of ill-treatment within the mill walls were well known in the locality and the Lingards and many other families must have consciously avoided sending their children to this den of pain and misery. Even though it would have provided an extra income, the working conditions would have meant it would have to be a very last resort, brought about through desperation.

By the time Robert Blincoe had completed his apprenticeship, Elizabeth Lingard had finished bearing children, having given birth to her 14th child four years earlier. Their house would have been seemingly crammed to the rafters with both parents and their 10 surviving children living under one roof. There are no records to show that any of the older children had married by this date, but it is possible that Mary, their eldest girl, was in service in one of the larger households that existed in the area. The older boys may also have had lodgings in other places but if they had followed tradition and economic necessity then there is a greater chance they were all living at home. Overcrowding brought many problems: hunger when crops failed to produce the required surplus, and disease and infection from insanitary conditions.

As 1813 drew to a close the weather turned cold and temperatures plummeted to below freezing for weeks on end. In the New Year winter brought with it some of the heaviest snows seen and by February it was so cold that the Thames froze over and the last of the 'Frost Fairs' took place. Spring brought only a little respite and was one of the coldest on record, with the conditions causing problems everywhere. Even summer was cold; following a brief warm spell towards the end of spring a false sense of optimism had arisen but as the cold had returned this was soon dashed. Crops failed to grow as they should have and famine was a real prospect. Autumn too failed to deliver a much-needed boost.

It was against this unhealthy background that Anthony Lingard the younger had been brought up, a life of hardship and death, of struggling to live from day-to-day and of constantly having to look over his shoulder in an effort to survive. The battle to survive and improve his lot would have been a driving factor in his actions. Survive is not too strong a word either, for many a person starved when times were hard and they had been that way all along, with the governing powers only adding to the distress that the whole country felt.

Yet Anthony Lingard was perhaps just a pawn in a far bigger game that was drawing towards a conclusion, and as 1814 came to a close and the New Year dawned who could have known or guessed that the callous actions of this young man would help to change the laws of a nation?

# THE TOLL HOUSE MURDER

January 1815 was a damp, uncomfortable, miserable month in the hills of Derbyshire. Even during the daytime the temperatures struggled on many occasions to get above freezing, and this on top of the already depressing month of December that had brought with it high winds and very heavy rainfall made the already poor conditions worse. Life trudged on as the days changed from wet to fair, and from fair to wet, yet the land was on many occasions covered in a thick blanket of fog that blotted out the landscape for miles around: an impenetrable wall that could obscure everything from sight and muffle all kinds of sounds.

By 15 January Anthony Lingard the younger seemed to be a troubled man. He was keeping a secret that was shared by only one other person and he needed to find a way out of the situation that he found himself in. Whether he planned it in advance or whether it was a spur-of-the-moment impulse we shall never know, but that night he left his home in Litton and made his way down the valley towards the cottages at Wardlow Mires. The sun and moon had long since set over the horizon, making the night a dark and uninviting place. It is possible that this was one of those nights where the land was blanketed in fog, thereby providing yet more anonymity to all those who ventured out that night for whatever reason. Maybe this was why Lingard decided to make his way towards the toll house that was kept by the widow Hannah Oliver, where each day she would take the toll payments from the travellers who passed through on their journeys. Hidden by the pitch black of the night, Lingard arrived at the toll bar and made his way inside, where he knew that Hannah would be alone. It is not known whether she invited him inside or whether he forced his way in for the hour was late, yet at the same time Hannah would most probably have known Lingard, for he was a local man and she would have seen him frequently. Some even said that they were having an illicit liaison, which, although possible, seems hard to believe because of their difference in ages, Lingard being 23 years old and Hannah 48. Maybe Lingard had been making advances towards the widow, for it might be that he saw in her a way out of his predicament. After all, there have been many people who have succumbed to the charms of a younger person either from flattery or through loneliness.

Once inside it seems a violent argument soon erupted, with the situation quickly getting out of hand and deteriorating into violence. With the strength of desperation, Hannah tried to fight off Lingard, and, as legend has it, at one time lashing out with a stick in an effort to beat him off, but his youthfulness prevailed and he managed to overpower the struggling toll keeper. The coup de grâce came when Lingard managed to pass a silk scarf around the widow's neck and with all his might tightened this silken noose until finally Hannah was dead. Lingard let Hannah's lifeless body fall to the floor and left her lying in a tangled heap just inside the toll house doorway.

Searching around, Lingard took just a few items that he could easily carry and that would be of use to him, these being 'several pounds in cash and notes' and, strangely enough, a new pair of red shoes that Hannah had only recently taken delivery of. But maybe they were not such an odd item to take after all, for Lingard had a use in mind for them and it could be that they were the reason behind his visit in the first place and that the theft of the money was simply a bonus. If the killing was pre-meditated or accidental will never be known, it could just have been an argument that got out of hand, but regardless of this Hannah's death would turn Lingard into a wanted man – assuming that he could be identified as the killer, that is. He knew that he had to keep a low profile and make sure no one knew of his whereabouts that night, and with that in mind he quietly slipped out of the toll house and into the all-embracing darkness outside. By a cruel twist of fate, Hannah Oliver's sister, who was also a toll keeper, but in her case on the Yorkshire Moors, also died at the hands of a murderer that very same night.

As morning came a commotion was heard outside the toll house, as travellers impatient to continue their journey waited with increasing anger for Hannah to take their money and allow them access onto the turnpike road. The noise of the angry crowd reached the ears of the barmaid from the inn nearby and quickly she made her way to seek out the cause of the rumpus. Making her way to the doorway of the toll house, she found the crumpled body of Hannah lying just beyond its threshold. Without delay, the constables were called and dutifully they began their investigations, taking statements and interviewing all those that could possibly shed any light on to the death of Hannah. The art of forensic science had yet to be discovered and any telltale signs that had been left by the killer would rely solely on the vigilance of the constables. With no formal training behind them, the upholders of the law had little chance of finding any clues, but they would have tried nonetheless. It was all to no avail, however, and already the trail was going cold, for there were no witnesses to the killing and the murderer had left no clues as to his or her identity. It looked as though the wheels of justice would grind slowly, or worse, not at all, for the authorities had no indication where to go next. The only hope they had was to find Hannah's missing red shoes and let them lead the way to the murderer.

As the constables were making their enquiries, Lingard was steadily making his way to the house of a young woman who lived in the area nearby. It was his visit to the young woman that would ultimately lead to his downfall, for he gave her Hannah's new red shoes and some money, and all he asked for in return was her silence. Not silence for the murder he had committed, for the young woman had no knowledge of it, but rather silence on a subject that had been troubling Lingard for some time and had led to his fatal actions. The woman he was visiting was pregnant with Lingard's child and he gave her the money and shoes that he had stolen from Hannah as a way of inducing her to claim that the child's father was someone other than himself. For whatever reason, whether it was greed, fear of Lingard, desperation or plain flattery, the young woman accepted his offer and kept both the money and the shoes. It was quite likely with a sigh of relief that Lingard left the house to make his way home, believing that he would never be found out as Hannah's murderer and that the young woman would not be pursuing him as the father of her child. Yet how can he have really thought that he would not be found out for Hannah's death? The only traceable item stolen from the toll house was Hannah's new pair of shoes and those he had given to a young woman in the very same area to where the victim had lived. Was Lingard so short-sighted and stupid or did he really think that the young woman would keep both of his secrets and that he would quite literally get away with murder?

It did not take long for the knowledge of Hannah Oliver's death to start spreading, and within the close-knit communities that pressed close by to the toll house the talk would have been all about how and why she had died. No doubt fear would have been felt by many, as they wondered who could have committed the crime and whether it would be safe to venture out while the murderer was still on the loose.

Then, as now, an unsolved crime perpetrated by an unknown criminal could make even the staunchest of characters worry as to their own safety and to contemplate the possibility that their neighbour was the guilty party. Within a short time, rumours of Hannah's murder and the theft of the red shoes began to reach the ears of Lingard's pregnant lover and she soon started to have worries and doubts about where the shoes had really come from. Without waiting, she gathered up the shoes and made her way to Lingard and confronted him about the gift. Lingard tried to calm the young woman by telling her that he had come by them legally and there was no need to be frightened as he had simply exchanged a pair of stockings for them in a fair transaction. The young woman refused to believe Lingard and made him take the shoes back. We shall never know if she thought that Lingard had come by the shoes by honest means or if he had anything to do with the death of Hannah Oliver; however, one thing for sure is that she had doubts and those doubts would ultimately seal Lingard's fate.

Fearing that the return of the shoes could implicate him in the murder if they were found, Lingard took them and hid them in a haystack. Yet even then he was having doubts about the wisdom as to the choice of hiding place and, fearing that the shoes could be easily found, he decided to move them. Making his way back to the haystack, he managed to retrieve the damning evidence and quickly made his way back to his own home. It could have been panic, desperation or fear at the thought of being caught, but Lingard's next choice of hiding place quite simply beggars belief for he hid them within the four walls of his own home, and some reports actually put the hiding place as his own bedroom.

As Lingard was hiding and re-hiding the shoes his lover was having doubts as to what to do next: should she keep silent or speak up? Soon she came to a decision and made her way to the local authorities. There she told her story of how she had been presented with a pair of shoes that were similar to those that had been taken from Hannah Oliver and how she had returned them to the person who had given them to her as a gift; how she had returned them to Anthony Lingard. The constables, grateful for a lead as to who the murderer could be, seized on the chance to interrogate the suspect and made their way with all due haste to the Lingard family home, where they eagerly questioned the potential killer about any possible involvement in Hannah Oliver's death. It was not an admission of guilt that sealed Lingard's fate, however, it was the discovery of Hannah Oliver's new red shoes that were found during a search of the property. For all his protestations of innocence, Lingard was taken into custody with the constables believing that the evidence they had found was sufficient to prove his guilt. But was it? There was no confession and the only evidence they had was the pair of shoes. Was Lingard's story about the exchange true after all? If he had taken part in an exchange then the shoes could no longer belong to Hannah Oliver for the swap must have taken place before the murder. The pressure would be on the authorities to show that these were indeed the victim's possessions, and with the absence of any form of forensics the task would be nigh-on impossible. Or would it?

Whoever was right, it would be up to a jury to decide guilt or innocence and so Lingard was taken to Derby and committed to gaol to await his fate.

# TRIAL AND EXECUTION

As the days passed slowly by, the date for Lingard's trial began to draw closer. The gaol would have started to become more and more crowded as prisoners awaiting trial were kept in its cramped conditions and the situation in the cells at times were almost intolerable. Many of those kept behind its walls were in fact given free range of its interior and yard, with only those causing trouble or likely to try to escape being shackled or, on a few very rare cases, double shackled. But even this relatively relaxed air could not hide the fact that the gaol only had seven cells and was designed to hold up to 21 prisoners, which meant a distinct lack of privacy at the best of times, and there were many occasions (usually in the lead-up to an assizes) when there could be four, five or even six prisoners to a cell, with each of these cells only just over 7ft square and a little over 8ft in height. Tempers would often be frayed, and at night time conditions within each of the cells would have been unbearable, with the only fresh air coming from a small vent above the cell door that faced onto the corridor. Even here, the air would be dank and still in this semi-subterranean place, where a small breeze would have brought the only relief from the stench of unwashed bodies kept in close confinement. With the date of the trial approaching, Lingard would have had plenty of time to reflect upon past happenings and to wonder if things could have turned out differently, but, regrettably, no record exists as to his thoughts or any of the conversations he had with his fellow inmates. We do know, however, that his behaviour left a lot to be desired and he showed little sign of remorse, behaving in a somewhat improper way, and generally it seems that he either did not realise the gravity of the situation he was in or he did not care. Perhaps he thought he would be acquitted, after all the only real evidence against him was that of the red shoes and to prove ownership looked an almost impossible task.

February came and went, and soon the days of March steadily passed, as gradually the date of the trial drew closer. As each day passed, Lingard and the other gaol inmates would have been treated to a bland repetitive gaol diet that did little for body or soul. The food that he had been eating while at home would have seemed like fine dining compared to the very simple fare that he had to put up with now – a miserable diet based around the staple of bread. Some would say that at least he was sure of getting a meal each day, and that is quite true, yet it is also true to say that it was not the sort of food he would have chosen had he been given the choice. Gaols were not meant to be a place of correction, they were a place of holding prisoners until they had been on trial and it was decided what to do with them, whether they be innocent or guilty. Those providing the funds to buy sustenance for inmates in the gaol did it under the premise of buying the food as cheaply as possible, with variety and quality being low down on the order of priorities.

At about 2 o'clock on 22 March 1815 the High Sherriff of the county, Sir Henry Fitzherbert, Baronet of Tissington, and a whole retinue of splendidly attired attendants arrived in Derby to take up their official duties in readiness for the forthcoming assizes. Almost immediately afterwards, they were joined by the Honourable Sir John Bayley, a much respected man, who would pass many judgements in the days to come, for he would be the trial judge and in many cases would have the power of life or death in his hands. Sir John was to have a successful career in the judiciary and would earn the greatly honoured title of privy councillor in years to come.

The judge began the official proceedings by opening his commission of assizes and, as was the custom, Sir John, Sir Henry Fitzherbert and the whole retinue then made their way to All Saints Church, where the Revd Alderson (who just happened to be Sir Henry's chaplain) gave a sermon based upon the verse 'And the fruit of righteousness is sown in peace of them that make peace'. It is apparent that the Revd Alderson not only wanted to do his job but also wanted to give succour to his superiors by justifying from the Bible any judgement that might be given in the days to come. The *Derby Mercury* was perhaps expressing the views of the day when it described the sermon as '…most excellent and appropriate…'

As the gathered gentry listened with varying degrees of interest to the devout clergyman delivering his piece, Lingard was languishing in gaol, awaiting his date with the courtroom, but he was probably already aware that the trial judge was in town. All the inmates would have been aware, for even with no official announcement to them the 'grapevine' was a very efficient means of communication. At about 4 o'clock Sir Henry, accompanied by a large party of his retinue, made their way to the George Inn where they all sat down to enjoy a rather sumptuous dinner, for gentlemen of that standing with the duties that they had to perform were entitled to fine food with decent and honourable company. Contrast this with the conditions and meals that the gaol inmates were provided with and the chasm between the classes begins to become even more apparent.

As a rule, prisoners awaiting trial today are presumed innocent until proven guilty, and so it was for Lingard and his compatriots, but there was a mentality that prevailed which said they were innocent until proven guilty, yet they probably were guilty anyway. Those in the gaol settled down for the night amid the tensions of the coming days, sleeping in the cramped, close, stinking conditions and surrounded by sweating bodies, trying as best they could to get some rest. For Sir John and Sir Henry it would have been plush surroundings and warm comfortable beds, with the finest food and drink. In the thinking of the day they had earned and deserved such things, and to be able to perform their duty to the best of their ability they were a necessity, hardly a privilege. Sir John settled down that night, knowing that in the morning he would be able to enjoy a hearty breakfast in readiness for the work ahead, because at 9 o'clock prompt the following morning the assizes would begin.

The whole of the first day was taken up with minor cases in which the erudite Sir John passed his judgements, with the main case of the day being a disagreement between Messrs Brown and Dawe over a disputed loan. Hardly the sort of case that would have stretched the learned gentleman's imagination, yet still one of importance that required his opinion and verdict. Tomorrow would bring more serious and much more important matters to the fore, matters that really would be a case of life and death for those accused. When the first day's work was finished, Sir John made his way back to his lodgings and once again took a refreshing meal and slept in a pleasant room, while yet again Lingard slept the sleep of a man about to go on trial for his life. Tomorrow was to be the day of his trial.

The following day Lingard was removed from the gaol on Friargate and taken under escort through the streets to the grand and imposing Shire Hall in St Mary's Gate where the assizes were held. In due course Lingard was brought into the courtroom itself and there in the dock he stood facing his accusers, with the judge Sir John Bayley, the jury and the packed public gallery all waiting for his story to be told. A murder trial has always caught the imagination of the public, especially one that held all the hallmarks of mystery and intrigue as this one did.

The prosecution had a number of witnesses to call against Lingard, yet there had been no witness to the murder itself, so a definite identification as to who the killer was would have appeared an impossibility. However, as the trial continued the circumstantial evidence continued to build. One of the most damning pieces of evidence came from the young woman who was carrying Lingard's unborn child; she told the story of how she had been presented with the red shoes and on hearing of Hannah Oliver's death had returned them to her lover. Even though he had tried to reassure her as to how he came by them she doubted his word and so contacted the authorities and explained all to them. Still, it had yet to be established whether the shoes that Lingard had offered were indeed those that had belonged to the victim; although soon the testimony of one man was to sink Lingard with no hope of reprieve. The prosecution called to the stand Samuel Marsden, a shoemaker from Stoney Middleton, a village some little distance from the scene of the murder, and it was he that confirmed the shoes as belonging to Hannah Oliver. But would one man's word be enough to condemn another to death because of an opinion as to ownership of a possession? The shoes themselves provided the all-important evidence, for each time Marsden was asked to make a pair of shoes he would include in the very material of the shoes a piece of paper and on that paper he would write a motto or piece of Biblical text, with each piece of text being different from the previous one. Marsden began to dismantle one of the shoes and there he found the paper he had inserted during the shoe's manufacture, a piece of paper that carried the prophetic words *'Commit no crime'*.

The prosecution closed its case against Lingard and allowed him to begin his non-existent defence, but he had no witnesses that he could call upon that could vouch in his favour, and so how could one simple countryman defend himself against the might of the judiciary? Lingard was doomed. The judge carefully summed up the evidence and directed the jury to make their decision. With such a one-sided case it took just a few minutes for a verdict to be reached, one which was undoubtedly guilty. The judge donned his black cap and, turning to Lingard, he passed the only sentence possible – death by hanging. In its time it was a sometimes cruel and painful death by slow strangulation and not the quick, painless death it was imagined to be by most. As was normal in these cases, the judge also directed that after death Lingard's body would be dissected and anatomised; in other words he would be carved up in order that the medical profession could learn more about the human body. The judge's direction as regards the dissection was not part of the sentence, for that was not within the scope of the sentencing allowed; however, after death the prisoner's body was forfeit to the state and it was this that allowed the judge's ruling. Sir John then implored Lingard to make the most of his remaining time and to prepare himself for '…the great change…' he was about to suffer.

The words of the judge do not appear to have had a great effect on Lingard, for even after being returned to Friargate, observers described his temperament as being 'obstinate', with no real signs of penitence being shown. Religious matters seem to have been completely above him and he showed little or maybe even no signs of being worried or agitated by his forthcoming death. The chances are that for the last few weeks he had been resigning himself more and more to his demise but there was still something within him that felt bitterness and hatred to others that he blamed for his predicament. While awaiting his time in the gaol, he admitted to the murder of Hannah Oliver, that at least would be off his conscience, but it was with great reluctance that he was able to say that he forgave the young woman who was carrying his child, for in his mind she was the reason that he was here; if she had not told the authorities about the shoes then all would have been different.

All the time that the condemned man sat within the gaol walls he would have heard the loud noises of hammers banging and workmen hard at work as they made the gallows for his execution. There was no way that he could hide from any of this activity, for the gallows were being made outside the gaol entrance itself, just feet away from where he was incarcerated. It was surely a type of mental torture as well, but again this did not appear to affect Lingard. Preparations were not only made within the area of the gaol for the forthcoming event, but also outside, as the traders would take advantage of the visiting crowds from whom great deal of money could be made. Executions were not only used as a public means of warning for wrongdoers, they were also a great social event and huge crowds could be expected. It had been two years since the last hanging in the area and 12 years since a murderer was sent to meet his maker so the turnout was expected to be good.

By the morning of 29 March everything was ready. The gallows were complete, all the traders were ready to sell their wares and the crowds had started to build. Since early morning the spectators had started to gather, after all, the earlier they arrived then the better vantage point they could command. It was a common practice that those with buildings overlooking the execution site would supplement their income and rent out the upstairs rooms to those who wished to have a better view of the proceedings. Amid all this activity the pickpockets would be at work, risking their own lives just to make some easy money in the closely packed crowds. Many of those in the crowd would have come for reasons other than to see justice done, or even to take part in a market atmosphere. To these people, the execution of a criminal could possibly give them or their child a chance of health.

Over many centuries superstitions had arisen about the health benefits that the body of an executed criminal could bestow on those lucky enough to be able to touch it. Pregnant or nursing women would jostle their way to the front of the crowd or form an impatient and exited queue ready to pay the hangman for the privilege of touching their bare breasts on to the body of the executed criminal. They believed that the sweat of the dead criminal contained their life force and this would be passed through the mother's milk and so protect their own children. Others would take their already sick child and hold them against the corpse in the hope that this would cure their illness as the life force passed directly into them. Those too impatient to wait would do their best to perform this task as the condemned was still kicking wildly in their death throes at the end of the rope. If someone had a skin blemish then it was regarded as sufficient to press the dead person's hand against the afflicted person's face. The hangman could and would use every opportunity to make money from his profession, and to supplement his income he would sell off pieces of rope and small pieces of the gallows, both of which were also assured to have healing properties.

It was a commonly held belief among those of the underworld that they would be able to continue their trade in secrecy if they possessed a 'hand of glory'. This macabre talisman could only be obtained by cutting off the hand of the newly executed criminal. If it was a murderer, the hand had to be the one that had done the deed, otherwise it was the left hand. After the hand had been dried and pickled, a candle was then made from the body fat, along with virgin wax and Lapland sesame seed oil. The candle was then placed into the grip of the pickled hand. It was believed that when a criminal took the hand of glory on a burglary or some other crime it would either render them invisible or make any witness motionless and unable to move. It was also thought that the light from this candle could only be put out with milk. It was a belief of invincibility based on myth and superstition; however, Anthony Lingard was not to suffer the fate of losing either hand.

Throughout his time spent in Friargate, Lingard would have had one frequent visitor, for it was the duty of the chaplain to prepare the condemned man to meet his maker. At midday on 29 March the chaplain, Lingard and a number of officials made their way to the newly erected gallows outside the main entrance to the gaol. The prisoner's arms were secured to his body using a strap or rope, leaving his hands free to carry any object he might desire, such as a Bible, for comfort. It used to be tradition that only the condemned prisoner's wrists were tied, but there had been some unfortunate cases where as the trapdoor opened to let the prisoner fall they threw out their arms and hung on as long as they could until, finally, exhaustion got the better of them and they let go. In one unfortunate case one man actually grabbed the rope by which he was being hanged and witnesses watched in horror as slowly he became more and more tired until at last he released his grip and suffered an even longer death as the rope slowly bit into his neck. Lingard would not be allowed to go through this, for him the sentence would be carried out as prescribed by law.

On the scaffold itself Lingard and the chaplain spent a short time in prayer together before a hood was pulled down over the prisoner's face, the noose placed around his neck and he was sent into oblivion in front of an excited crowd. There are no records to say whether he died quickly or slowly, but it was the custom of the day for reports to say that the end came quickly – even though this was a rare occurrence – simply because to tell the truth about how long the prisoner hanged before expiring might upset the reading populace. It was said that Lingard met his end with a resoluteness that would under normal circumstances have been admired, but once again it was normal for reporters to express this opinion so that it would appear the criminal was contrite for their crimes. Quite likely Lingard was resigned to his fate and this gave the appearance of resolution in his prospect rather than true penitence. It is doubtful if any of his family visited him while in gaol but if they did then this might be the cause of his apparent change in attitude.

After hanging the required length of time, Lingard's body was cut down, but instead of being sent to the Shire Hall for dissection his body was sent away for a different purpose. Before Sir John left town he had a change of heart and instead of allowing the body to be dissected he ordered that the body of Lingard be gibbeted at a place as close to the murder as possible. Gibbeting of a body was a practice that was becoming increasingly rare by 1815, yet some people believed it served its purpose as a deterrent to other would-be criminals. The body of the newly executed prisoner would be taken away and sheathed in a casing of canvas. This would then be coated in tar and finally it would be encased in a body-shaped cage of steel or chains. The body and its coverings would then be displayed hanging from a wooden frame, usually about 30ft high, at a spot close to where the original crime took place. The canvas and tar were used as a preservative so that the body would not decompose. There are recorded incidents of bodies being gibbeted and buffeted by the elements for decades and this was the fate that the body of Lingard was destined to suffer.

The gibbeting of a criminal's body was seen as another opportunity for the ill and superstitious to obtain some form of relief for body and soul, for just as at executions it was believed that the malefactor could bring more good to the world now they were dead than when they were in the land of the living. The gibbet post itself was traditionally protected with nails or spikes that were driven into its sides to prevent trophy hunters climbing it to remove parts of the body, and also to stop friends or relatives from retrieving the body for secret burial. This did not stop the more determined or patient ones from achieving their goal, however. The skull was a much prized possession to have, for it was claimed that if a sufferer of epilepsy drank from it they would find it had curative properties. Those not able to reach the body would take small pieces of the gibbet itself to be used in cures. In 1650 Sir Thomas Browne noted that if some of the wood was worn as an amulet it would act as a cure for ague – an ancient term for a fever with chills and sweating. By the 19th century this type of remedy had spread to include relief from toothache.

# A WARNING TO OTHERS

In the case of Anthony Lingard the process of preparing his body for gibbeting was done with all due haste and word had already been sent ahead to make preparations for the arrival of the corpse at Wardlow Mires so that it could be displayed close to the toll house. The local constable, Sampson Hodgkinson, was already taking precautions that he felt would be needed to control the huge crowd of sightseers that he expected. He quite rightly decided that he would need help and so managed to get Sampson Wager and John Thornhill sworn in as constables also. Little did they know, however, that it would be a whole year before they received their payment for the services they had rendered, for then, as now, payments from governments and official bodies could be slow in coming. For two days' work they would each receive 16 shillings (80p) and more than likely a good story that they could recant to all those that were interested enough to listen on how they had officiated at one of the last public spectacles of its kind ever to be held in this country. As Wager and Thornhill were being sworn in, workmen were busily erecting the gibbet post in full knowledge that it would be expected to remain there for many years. Others too were making preparations for the spectacle that was coming to the area as this was a good time to try to make some money by erecting stalls to sell goods to all the visitors that would flood into the area. A good hanging always brought out the crowds but a gibbeting was a rare sight indeed and would make quite a difference to the local area, with tourists coming from far and wide even at such short notice.

As all this activity was taking place, Lingard's body was being covered in the canvas and tar before finally being encased in the metal frame that would keep it protected for many years and ensure that it remained on view as a deterrent for any would-be criminals. By Friday morning the body had been prepared and was ready for its final journey. To make sure that all went well, it had been entrusted to the army for transportation and so within a short time this unusual little cortège was on its way. It has always been assumed that professional bodies such as the armed forces are efficient and able to undertake any task that is given to them, and so it was on this particular occasion; however, it was not expected that the soldiers in charge of Lingard's body would make a simple but very important mistake. Making their way from Derby, they headed in the direction of Wardlow Mires (or so they hoped). Arriving at Rowsley, they became lost, took the wrong road and ended up passing through the Chatsworth Park. A popular story from that time states that the road was private and anyone using transport to pass over it was obliged to pay a toll, not a monetary payment but a nominal or symbolic payment of a tack or nail driven into one of the gateposts. The soldiers, however, did not perform this task, either through ignorance of the custom or laziness, and continued on towards the gibbeting site. Later, word spread of this oversight and someone invoked an old and ancient law that said if a dead body passed over a private road it automatically became a public road, giving free access and passage to all that chose to use it. Sadly, this tale is a just another myth surrounding the story of Anthony Lingard, as that particular road had been open to the public since at least 1770.

Late that day the soldiers and the gruesome cargo they protected arrived at Wardlow Mires, but already it was too late for the gibbeting to take place so the body of Lingard was placed in a nearby barn in readiness for the raising of the corpse after the next sunrise.

Saturday 1 April 1815 was to be a very important day for the populace of the area. From all around, sightseers came to watch as Lingard's body was hauled up and suspended high upon the gibbet post. More and more traders came and set up their stalls. There would have been stalls to sell food, stalls to sell all sorts of things for house and home, and as was normal there were more than likely stalls that sold mementos or trinkets that could be kept as a keepsake of the day. The whole scene was that of a fairground, and a fair in the countryside during the early 19th century was a welcome relief from the drudgery and hardship of trying to keep food on the table.

For the time of year the weather was exceptionally warm and the temperature steadily rose throughout the day, making the scene feel even more like a holiday and no doubt tempting yet more visitors to venture out and get a taste of the atmosphere and witness something that was unique within the area. As the morning wore on and merged into afternoon, the crowds continued to flock to see the macabre sight of this metal-clad, canvas-covered body as it swung gently overhead, and as the evening approached slowly the crowds began to disperse.

Legend has it that as the afternoon died away one man came especially to witness for himself Lingard's body suspended from the gibbet post and he gazed with sadness at the fate that had befallen this young man, for this was Anthony Lingard the elder, who had braved the crowds to see his son. One other man was watching this scene and he watched Anthony Lingard the elder with sorrow and sympathy, for he believed that for all the faults and failings of Lingard the younger, he had paid his dues for the crime he had committed and the gibbeting of his body was something that should be condemned.

This elderly gentleman was William Newton, the manager of the nearby mill at Cressbrook, the same man that had been a partner to Ellis Needham at Litton Mill all those years ago. At Cressbrook he practised a more enlightened attitude to employing young people, and perhaps his experiences at Litton Mill had taught him some valuable lessons in the treatment of those not so fortunate as himself. Newton was born in 1750 at Abney in Derbyshire and was baptised at Hope (both villages were not too distant from his present location) on Christmas Day that same year, ironically the same day of the year that

Lingard the elder and his wife were married all those years later. Thankfully for Newton, his life had not followed the same troubled path. After having a varied career – at one time he was the landlord of an inn and at another was even declared bankrupt – he became manager at Cressbrook in 1810 and there he was able to implement some of the more humane methods of work that he believed in. In contrast to conditions in other mills, those practised at his own were regarded as relatively humane and he is remembered as treating many of his younger employees as his extended family. For all the good things that he did, Newton was not perfect and he did at times work his employees hard; however, through all this he did appear to have a basically kind nature. His reputation at the time was such that he was called 'The Minstrel of the Peak' by the writer Anna Seward[1], who not only liked him for who he was but also admired his writings, for he was a much regarded poet as well.

The sight of Anthony Lingard the elder watching the body of his son being put on display and open to ridicule was something that Newton found distressing and in his own way he felt he had to do something. There was a general feeling at that time that gibbeting was a practice that ought to be abolished and the mood of the country was swinging behind the abolitionists. Indeed, the practice of gibbeting was becoming more and more rare and that is possibly why this particular morbid event was attracting such a large crowd. Some time later Newton penned a very poignant poem that summed up the sight of Anthony

Lingard the elder as he watched with sadness the demise of his beloved son. The beginning of this poem brings to life the agony that Lingard the elder must have suffered.

*Time: MIDNIGHT. Scene: A STORM*

*ART thou, my Son, suspended here on high?*
*Ah! What a sight to meet a Father's eye!*
*To see what most I prized, what most I loved,*
*What most I cherish'd – and once most approved,*
*Hung in mid air to feed the nauseous worm,*
*And waving horrid in the midnight storm!*

*Let me be calm; – down, down, my swelling soul;*
*Ye winds, be still – ye thunders, cease to roll!*
*No! ye fierce winds, in all your fury rage;*
*Ye thunders, roll; ye elements, engage;*
*O'er me be all your mutual terrors spread,*
*And tear the thin hairs from my frenzied head:*[2]

As poignant as it was, it was not just the sight of Lingard's cocooned body that inspired Newton to put pen to paper and express in the best way he knew his feelings on gibbeting, there was also a letter that had been written by Spence Broughton, a man convicted of robbing the mail near Sheffield, to his wife Eliza in April 1792 that finally influenced him to act. Written

The 1791 baptism record for Anthony Lingard the younger, who grew up to be a murderer. (Derbyshire Records Office D1494 A/PI 1/4)

The burial entries for 1797 showing that the Lingard family suffered more than their neighbours. A notation deep in the right-hand margin and mainly hidden explains the deaths were from smallpox. (Derbyshire Records Office D1494 A/Pl 1/5)

No. 250

James Warhirst of [the] Parish of Tideswell
and Ellen Palfreeman of [the]
same parish, Spinster were
Married in this [Church] by [Banns] publishd three several Sundays
this twenty eight Day of Nov in the Year One Thousand seven Hundred
and eighty Six by me Rich: Shuttleworth — Vicar
This Marriage was { James Warhirst
solemnized between Us, { Ellen Palfreeman + her mark
In the { Benj: Baker
Presence of { Francis Palfreeman

No. 251

Rob: Longston of [the] Parish of Tideswell
and Nancy Wood of [the]
Parish of Chapel-en-le-frith Spinster were
Married in this [Church] by [Banns]
this fourteenth Day of Dec in the Year One Thousand Seven Hundred
and Eighty Six by me Rich: Shuttleworth Vicar
This Marriage was { Robert Longston his mark
solemnized between Us { Nancy Wood + her mark
In the { Saml Slack
Presence of { Joseph Longson

No. 252

Rob: Hurstone of [the] Parish of Tideswell
and Hannah Townsend of [the]
Same Parish, Spinster were
Married in this [Church] by [Banns] butteshid 3 several Sundays 41
this twenty fourth Day of Dec in the Year One Thousand seven Hundred
and Eighty Six by me Rich: Shuttleworth
This Marriage was { Robert Hurstone
solemnized between Us { Hannah + Townsend her Mark
In the { Wm Gibson Junr
Presence of { Wm Townsend

No. 253

Anthony Lingard of [this] Parish
and Elizabeth Neal of [the]
same parish Spinster were
Married in this [Church] by [Banns published 3 several Sundays
this twenty fifth Day of Dec in the Year One Thousand seven Hundred
and Eighty Six by me Rich: Shuttleworth
This Marriage was { Anthony Lingard his mark
solemnized between Us { Elizabeth Neal + her mark
In the { Richard Leech
Presence of { John Lingard

Anthony Lingard and Elizabeth Neal's marriage record for Christmas Day 1786. One of the witnesses was John Lingard, possibly his father but more probably his brother. (Derbyshire Records Office D1494 A/Pl 3/2)

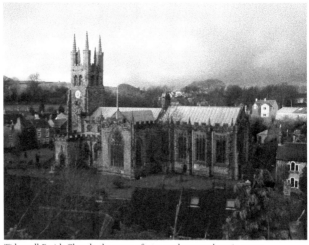

Tideswell Parish Church, the scene of so many happy and tragic events.

The interior of Tidewell Parish Church. It was here where Anthony Lingard the elder and Elizabeth Neal were married, all their children were baptised and where ultimately a number of them had their funerals, along with William Newton and the murder victim Jane Grant.

Litton village, which produced two murderers and a highway robber in just a few short years.

Litton. The road leading to Wardlow Mires with the possible Lingard house in the centre.

The road from Tideswell to Litton.

No one knows which house in Litton the Lingard family lived in, and a number of dwellings claim that accolade, but local oral legend says this cottage could be one of them.

Litton Lane End Farm. There is no definitive proof as to where the Lingard family lived but this farm fits the bill in many ways. Not only does it overlook the site of the toll house, but it also bears the same name as the farm the Lingards supposedly lived in. The ownership of the farm can be traced from 1763 to the present day – except for the period when the Lingards would have been there.

The new road through Stoney Middleton leading to Lover's Leap. Anthony Lingard's body was taken along the road which runs behind the buildings on the left.

The Three Stags' Heads Inn (formerly the Devonshire Arms) at Wardlow Mires. It was from within this inn that the barmaid ventured forth to seek the cause of the commotion outside and soon found the murdered Hannah Oliver in the nearby toll house. This is also one of the two possible locations at which John Bagshaw stopped to take refreshments before being attacked by William Lingard and William Bennet.

Graffiti done by prisoners on the cell doors of Derby gaol.

One of the cramped cells in Derby gaol where it was not unusual to have up to four, five or even six prisoners squeezed in.

The entrance to one of the cells in Derby gaol, which retains the original door.

The bridge at the south entrance to Chatsworth Park over which Anthony Lingard's body was taken on its way to be gibbeted.

The road through the Chatsworth estate over which Anthony Lingard's body was carried.

The water mill on the Chatsworth estate past which Lingard's body and its army escort passed on the way to Wardlow Mires.

Chatsworth House. Legend has it that in the late 17th century the Duke of Devonshire had live gibbeting abolished because he was being disturbed and kept awake by the cries and screams of a murderer being gibbeted alive on the moor behind the house.

This barn at the side of the Three Stags' Heads Inn at Wardlow Mires is reputedly the one in which Anthony Lingard's body was kept overnight before the gibbeting.

The view from near Benstor (Denston) Bottoms looking towards Wardlow Mires and the gibbet site.

The gibbeting irons of John Breads. In 1742 John Breads was executed for stabbing the mayor of Rye – his skull is still in place in the irons. Anthony Lingard's body was encased in a frame of much the same design. (Rye Town Council)

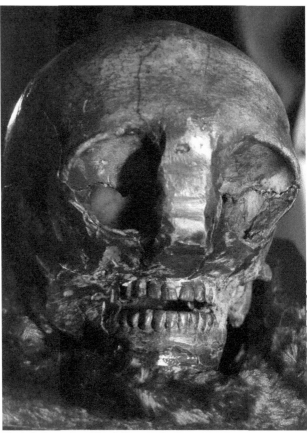

The skull of a murderer. This skull on display at Littledean jail in Gloucestershire is thought to be that of the executed Anthony Lingard. The rather grotesque and crude lower jaw and teeth were added many years ago to add a sense of completeness and to make it more of a curiosity.

(Kind permission of Jules Annan/
Concertphotography.co.uk)

BURIALS in the Parish of _Tideswell_ in the County of _Derby_ in the Year 18_18_

| Name. | Abode. | When buried. | Age. | By whom the Ceremony was performed. |
|---|---|---|---|---|
| Tho* Hall, Son of Rob* & Ellen No. 305. | Litton | Aug* 19* | 46 yrs | Tho* Brown Vicar of Tideswell |
| Charles Son of Will* & Ann Cotton No. 306. | Tideswell | Aug* 23. | 3¾ yrs | Tho* Brown Vicar of Tideswell |
| Sarah Walton Widow No. 307. | Tideswell | Sept* 1 | 64 yrs | Tho* Brown Vicar of Tideswell |
| Martha, Daug* of W* & Martha Middleton No. 308. | Tideswell | Sept* 16* | 2 weeks | Tho* Brown Vicar of Tideswell |
| Ann, Wife of James Bagshaw No. 309. | Grindlow | Sept* 18. | 79 yrs | Tho* Brown Vicar of Tideswell |
| Jane, Daug* of Jane Grant No. 310. | Litton | Sept* 19 | 21 yrs | Tho* Brown Vicar of Tideswell |
| Hannah, Daug* of Godfrey & Sarah Dawson No. 311. | Tideswell | Sept* 24 | 2 weeks | Tho* Brown Vicar of Tideswell |
| Sarah, illeg. Daug* of Mary Curtbidge No. 312. | Tideswell | Sept* 27 | 11 months | Tho* Brown Vicar of Tideswell |

When Jane Grant was laid to rest on 19 Septmeber 1818 her mother was bidding farewell to her second child to die prematurely. The entry was later amended to include the much-faded words 'Poisoned wilfully by arsenic by Hannah Bocking, who was executed at Derby 22<sup>nd</sup> March 1819'. (Derbyshire Records Office D1494 A/Pl 5/1)

The site of the gibbet at Wardlow Mires, which is also the place where Hannah Bocking gave Jane Grant the poisoned cake.

The former George Hotel in Derby. This building has played a significant part in the history of Derby. In 1745 it was the headquarters for the Duke of Devonshire as he prepared to repel the army of Bonnie Prince Charlie; it was also where the van of the rebel army arrived demanding billets for their men. Latterly it became the hotel where members of the judiciary (including Sir John Bailey and his fellow judges) would rest in comfort while those in the gaol waited in stinking, acrid conditions.

The site of the Friargate gaol in Derby, in front of which Anthony Lingard and Hannah Bocking were executed.

The Shire Hall in Derby where the trials of both the Lingard brothers, Hannah Bocking and William Bennet took place. It was also where Hannah Bocking's body was publicly dissected after her execution.

*Hannah Bock[ing]*
*his in this Callin[der]*

# SENTENCES OF THE FELON PRISON[ERS]

*Confined in His Majesty's Gaol for the County of Derby, who have taken their Trials before the Right [Honourable]* ROBERT DALLAS, *Knight, Lord Chief Justice of our said Lord the King of his Court of Common [Pleas; and the] Honourable Sir* JAMES BURROUGH, *Knight, one other of the Justices of our said Lord the King of [his Court] of Common Pleas, at the Assizes for the County of Derby, held at the County Hall, in Derby, on [the] 17th Day of March, 1819.*

### EDWARD COKE, OF LONGFORD, ESQ. HIGH-SHERIFF.

SOPHIA WIGLEY, aged 21, and BRIDGET DERWARE, aged 18, charged with stealing at Ashborne, a quantity of buff kerseymere and other articles, the property of Charles Haywood. Committed August 3, 1818, by W. Webster, Esq.— Committed, but reprieved.

JOHN GIBSON, aged 19, Charged with breaking into the dwelling-house of William Webb, of Findern, and stealing thereout ten yards of flannel. Committed August 28, 1818, by Bache Heathcote, Esq. Condemned but reprieved.

HANNAH BOCKING, aged 16, charged with feloniously poisoning Jane Grant, the younger, at Litton. Committed September 19, 1818, by James Mander, Esq. Coroner. Guilty Death, and to be Executed on Monday, and her body to be given to the Surgeons for Dissection. *Hanged March 22 1819 Monday*

JOSEPH BERESFORD, aged 27, and G. TURNER, jun. aged 23, charged with feloniously killing and slaying Isaac Smith, at Sheldon. Committed October 7, 1818, by James Mander, Esq. Coroner. Joseph Beresford to be imprisoned 9 months, and George Turner, junr. 4 months.

BENJAMIN PEACH, aged 32, charged with breaking into the dwelling-house of John Pratt, at Bradby, and stealing eight promissory notes of the value of two pounds each; and other articles. Committed October 19, 1818, by Sir Oswald Mosley, bart. and A. N. Mosley, Esq. Acquitted.

JOHN LOUD, aged 19, charged with breaking into the dwelling house of Wm. Limb, in Chesterfield, and stealing nine yards of cloth and other articles. Committed October 23, 1818, by J. Elam, Esq. Condemned, but repr'ved.

JOSEPH BAILEY, aged 39, charged with stealing out of the pocket of Joseph Hallam, at Alsop, a leather case, containing a five guinea bill and two Macclesfield notes. Committed Nov. 14, 1818, by S. Frith, Esq. One year.

GEORGE SELLORS, aged 54, and PETER JONES, aged 64, charged with stealing out of the pocket of Thomas Hall, on the King's highway at Hope, twenty-seven one pound bank of England notes, his property. Committed Nov. 14, 1818, by Sir C. W. Bagshaw, and S. Frith, Esq. both acquitted

JOHN DUFFIELD, aged 39, charged with stealing a black ewe sheep, the property of the Rev. H. C. Morewood, of Alfreton. Committed Nov. 27, 1818 by W. Hilton, Esq. Condemned, but reprieved.

JOSEPH BOHAM, aged 47, charged with setting fire to a house in his possession, situate at Middleton and Smerrill. Committed December 26, 1818 by Sir M. Blakiston, Sir Henry Fitzherbert, bart. and W. Webster, Esq. Acquitted.

JAMES ILIFFE, aged 24, and MARK ILIFFE, aged 12, charged with stealing one sheep, in Belton, the property of John Chatterton. Committed Jan. 1, 1819, by D. P. Coke, Esq. Acquitted. Condemned, but reprieved.

WILLIAM WHITE, aged 16, and JOB RODGERS, aged 20, charged with robbing and violently assaulting Corn Pius Woodward, on the highway between Barlborough and Staveley. Committed January 19, 19 by J. Jebb, Esq. Condemned, but reprieved.

JOHN FOWKE, aged 40, charged with stealing and carrying away a quantity of potatoes, at Quarndon, the property of John C—, Esq. Committed Jan. 23, 1819 by D. P. Coke, Esq.—Six Months imprisonment.

WILLIAM ROBINSON, aged 45, charged with stealing out of a dwelling-house at Clifton, two pairs of men's shoes and a cotton jacket, the property of Humphrey Broughton. Committed January 29, 1819, by Sir M. Blakiston, and Sir Henry Fitzherbert, Bart., — Wynter, and R. Arkwright, jun. Esqr. Transported 7 years.

WILLIAM CORBRIDGE, aged 20, and JAMES MILLS, aged 10, charged with stealing a quantity of sheep iron, and other articles, the property of Francis Clough. Committed Feb. 9, 1819, by Sir W. G. Bagshaw.—One [year?]

SAMUEL EVANS, aged 30, charged with breaking into a dwelling-house at Dayton Bridge, and stealing thereout 100 guineas in gold, ten pounds in notes, six ounces in silver, and four seven-shilling pieces, the property of Samuel Hereford. Committed February 16, 1819, by W. Webster, Esq.—Condemned, but reprieved.

JOB BUNTING, aged 23, charged with defrauding at Ashford, of a horse, the property of John Redfern, of Tissington. Committed Feb. 3, 1819, by the Revnd Henry Fitzherbert, bart. Acquitted.

JOHN TURNER, aged 21, LEAH ALSEBROOK, aged [..] KENT, aged 66, the said John Turner is charged with stealing out buildings of Martin Massey, of Hilton, four geese, six fowls, and Leah Alsebrook and Samuel Kent, for receiving the same, knowing them to be stolen. Committed February 15 1819, by Sir Oswald Mosley, Esq—John Turner and Leah Alsebrook 6 months each Acquitted.

JOHN PLIMMER, aged 19, B. HOLMES, aged 19, and G[..] aged 67, the said John Plimmer and Benjamin Holmes for breaking into the house of Samuel Bridges, at Belper, in the night, and stealing a quantity of butter, cheese, flour, meat, and pork; and the said Garvis Holmes for taking part of the same, knowing them to have been stolen. Committed by John Radford, Esq. John Plimmer admitted evidence, Benjamin Holmes and Garvis Holmes, acquitted.

JAMES THOMPSON, aged 27; charged with stealing out of a quantity of raw hemp, the property of J. Jackson. Committed Dec 19, 1819, by D. P. Coke, Esq. Acquitted.

THOMAS HOPKINSON, jun. aged 20, and JOHN PLIMMER, charged with stopping William Bucknall upon the turnpike road, bodily fear, and taking from his person a purse containing two pounds. Committed February 20, 1819, by D. P. Coke, Esq.—Guilty.—Death, and John Fletcher recommended to mercy.

CHARLES SMEDLEY, aged 33, charged with stealing at Kirk Langley, the property of Thomas Frizer. Committed February 25, 1819, by G. Mowe ll, Esq. Acquitted.

JOHN SANDOM, jun. aged 27, J. SANDOM, aged 25, DOM, sen. aged 70, the said John Sandom the younger, is charged with stealing from a barn at Heage, four ricks and up the chaff, the property of John Wainwright; and the said John Sandom receiving the same, knowing it to have been stolen. Committed by J. Radford, Esq. Acquitted.

JOSHUA FLETCHER, charged with stealing five fowls, the property of John Marriott. Committed February 28, 1819, by J. R. No Bill returned.

THOMAS OAKLEY, aged 11, charged with stealing from Taylor, at Melborne, about 10s. weight of iron. Committed by D. P. Coke, Esq. No Bill.

JOHN RAGG alias JACK RAG, aged 32, and MARY [..], charged with stealing at Cubley, three geese and five fowls, the property of James Aistlewhorth. Mary Cotton admitted evidence, John Ragg acquitted.

HANNAH YEOMANS, aged 24, charged with stealing at [..] two pair of stockings, one handkerchief, two caps, three frills, and a flannel petticoat, the property of Mark Whitworth. [..]

WILLIAM ALEXANDER, aged 18, A. LEGGATT, LEGGETT, aged 34, and WILLIAM TAYLOR, aged 16, several articles of wearing apparel, of the value of 40s and [..] dwelling house of Joseph Spencer. The three former Committed admitted Evidence.

AARON HALL, JOSEPH KNOWLES, and JAMES [..] by Order of Court Martial, the said Aaron Hall for One Month ment, the other two for Two Months each.

## REMAIN IN CUSTODY.

Samuel Hudson, John Moore, John Morley, and George Taylor, two years ; Thomas Bunney, eighteen months in the House of Correction [..]

Gonalston Mill (formerly Cliffe Mill), near Loudham, was originally owned by Messer's Lambert and was where Robert Blincoe and his friends 'volunteered' to work.

The mill race at Gonalston Mill.

Gonalston village.

Cromford. While being transported from Lowdham to Litton Mill, Blincoe and the other apprentices were made to walk through the village by the overseer to show how healthy they were.

Willersley Castle at Cromford. This is the house that Richard Arkwright had built and which Blincoe and his friends passed close by on their way to Litton Mill.

Litton Mill. Ellis Needham's mill was all but destroyed by fire and a new one was built on the same site, with just a few fragments of the original remaining.

Litton Mill seen from the river.

One of the entrance gate posts to Litton Mill.

The River that leads to Litton Mill and provided its power. This is a sight that Robert Blincoe and the other apprentices would have known well.

The former Bulls Head Inn at Eyam, where Robert Blincoe went to see the magistrates.

The much-altered and renovated Cressbrook Mill where Willaim Newton implemented some of the more humane methods of employing mill workers.

The gravestone of William Newton at Tideswell Parish Church. Jane Grant who was murdered by Hannah Bocking, lies within the same graveyard but sadly she has no headstone.

The Anchor public house near Tideswell. This could have been the ale house that John Bagshaw rested in before making his way home after attending Litton market and where he first saw William Lingard and William Bennett.

Near Benstor (Denston) Bottoms, close to where Lingard and Bennett robbed John Bagshaw.

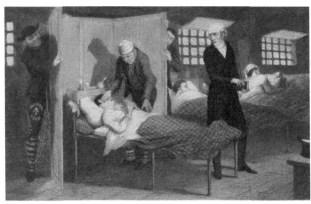

*Death of a convict on a hulk ship.* This painting from the 1830s shows that life on a hulk ship could be short. In fact, the conditions portrayed are much better than those in reality. The space between decks would be filthy, smelly, dark and with little headroom. Note the name 'Justitia' on the leg of the prisoner to the left of the picture. (National Library of Australia)

This picture of life around a hulk ship dates from about 1829 and shows a hulk ship in Portsmouth harbour. The convicts in the small boat would have hated and loathed the prospect of boarding the hulk after the relative freedom away from its cramped conditions for at least a short time. (National Library of Australia)

*A View from near Woolich in Kent, shewing (sic) the employment of convicts from the hulks.* Painted 1790–1800, the title says it all. Bennett and Lingard would have been part of a scene much like this one when they were incarcerated onboard the *Justitia* at Woolich while they awaited transportation. (National Library of Australia)

Replica of a convict uniform worn by prisoners in Australia from 1830 to 1849. The alternating yellow and black quartering was designed to make the convict stand out. (National Library of Australia)

Replica of the wollen and leather caps worn by convicts from 1830 to 1849. (National Library of Australia)

A 19th-century wood engraving of the whaling ship *Emily Downing*, formerly the convict ship *Lady Franklin*. (State Library of Victoria.)

The convict ship *Lady Franklin* on which William Lingard was transported from Norfolk Island to Hobart. (State Library of Victoria)

*Hyde Park Barracks.* William Lingard and William Bennett were kept here after their arrival in Australia. Every detail of their appearance and skills was recorded for further use so that their employment could be arranged, and should they escape a description could be circulated. (National Library of Australia)

William Lingard's attitude to authority and the problems that ensued led him to be part of a chain gang very much like this one. Life in a chain gang was hard and not for the faint hearted. (National Library of Australia)

Gallows gate on Norfolk Island in about 1909. (State Library of Victoria)

The prison establishment on Norkfolk Island in about 1909. (State Library of Victoria)

The Snake Pass Inn. When John Longden became landlord he took the opportunity to preach to his customers as often as he could, whom he no doubt treated as a captive audience. The Longden family were landlords at the Snake Inn for 58 years.

Stoney Middleton, from where Samual Marsden the shoemaker came.

A broadsheet giving the life story and final demise of Thomas Hopkinson. The woodcut print at the top of the page was far from accurate simply because the printer would choose from a selection of already cut scenes. In many cases the broadsheets were printed before the executions even took place.

Lover's Leap in Stoney Middleton. In 1762 (the year after Elizabeth Neal and Anthony Lingard the elder were born) Hannah Baddeley threw herself off the cliff after being jilted by her lover William Barnsley. She survived thanks to sturdy clothing and thick bushes, only to die of natural causes two years later.

### THE LIFE AND EXECUTION OF
# THOMAS HOPKINSON, jun.
Who suffered this Day on the New Drop, in front of the County Gaol, Derby,

## For Highway Robbery.

THIS unfortunate young man, only 20 years of age, was found guilty at the late Assizes in Derby, together with John Fletcher, of stopping William Bucknall upon the Turnpike Road near Dronfield, putting him in bodily fear, and taking from his person, a purse containing twelve shillings and six-pence.

The Criminal was born at Ashover, in this County, where he resided with his Father till he was fourteen years old. The family then removed to Woolley Moor, and here it was that he formed an intercourse with abandoned companions, and commenced that prodigate career which brought him to his untimely end. In the number of his wicked associates were Thomas Jackson, jun. John King, John Brown, and George Booth, who were all executed two years ago for setting fire to stacks of hay and corn in the farm-yard of Colonel Halton. Thomas Hopkinson was an accomplice in this horrid crime, and was admitted King's evidence on the trial of his companions. Their dreadful fate afforded no salutary warning to Hopkinson, who proceeded in his guilty career till he committed the crime for which the judgment of the law has thus been awfully executed upon him.

His life, though a comparatively short one, has been marked by the commission of an incredible number of offences. Of these he made a confession during his confinement in the house of correction at Chesterfield, and these are more than sufficient to shew that his whole time was spent in the perpetration of almost every species of vice. The petty pilferings in which he first engaged, gradually led him on to bolder offences; his mind became so familiarised with guilt, that he seemed scarcely sensible of its depravity; and thus in the natural progress of iniquity, he was led on till he "was driven away in his wickedness."

On looking back to the history of his short but criminal course, his first transgressions may with great justice be referred to the wicked company of Thomas Jackson, who was his constant associate. After this intimacy had been formed, every moral feeling and every religious consideration were abandoned. He no longer read his bible, he no longer went to church; and thus the seeds of instruction which had been sown in his infant mind were choked and became unfruitful. Poaching, robbing hen roosts, gardens, and barns were the occupations of his nights; and his days were spent either in that kind of idleness which is ever the fruitful source of fresh crimes, or in dissipating in profligate excess the money acquired by his nefarious practices. Offences of a still heavier kind succeeded of course to those we have enumerated. Sheep stealing, horse stealing, house breaking, and highway robbery, marked the boldness with which he and his companions advanced in vice. They were indeed the terror and the reproach of their neighbourhood. After his condemnation, Hopkinson showed not much concern for his approaching fate. The sight of the unfortunate woman in the chapel, who was going to be executed on the 22nd of March, excited in him a stronger emotion than he expressed on any other account, but he was not capable of deep reflection, and seldom seemed sufficiently impressed with the awful situation in which he himself was placed.

It is an uncommon thing for persons, who come to an untimely and disgraceful end, to acknowledge upon the fatal scaffold, that a neglect of the Sabbath, laid the foundation of their ruin.

Between twelve and one o'clock this day, he was brought to the fatal spot, and having spent a short time in prayer, he was launched into eternity, amidst a vast concourse of spectators.

(G. WILKINS, PRINTER, QUEEN STREET, DERBY.)

April 2d, 1819.

from his cell in York Castle, Broughton tells of his regret at leaving his wife and family to the mercies of society now that he is to die, and he expresses his sadness that his body will never have a resting place. Broughton was the last man to be gibbeted in Yorkshire and his corpse was put on public display in Sheffield for all to see for many years. It was this sad and tearful letter combined with the sight of Anthony Lingard the elder standing on the lonely hillside that influenced William Newton to act. The letter itself is a testament to the fear that such an end could instil in those who are sentenced to such a demise.

*York Castle,*
*April 14th 1792.*

*My Dear Eliza,*

     *This is the last affectionate token thou wilt ever receive from my hand, a hand that trembles at my approaching desolation, so soon, so very soon to ensue, before thou wilt open this last epistle of thy unfortunate husband, these eyes, which now overflow with tears of contrition, shall have ceased to weep, and this heart now fluttering on the verge of eternity, shall beat no more; I have prepared my mind to meet death without fear, And ah how happy, had that been the common visitation of nature; Be not discomforted, God will be your friend, in the solitude of my cell I have sought him, and his spirit hath supported me, hath assisted me in my prayers, and many a time in the moments of remorseful anguish, hath whispered peace for my dear Eliza, I never added cruelty to injustice. Yet I have resolved to meet death without fear.* [3]

It was either the same day as the gibbeting, or more than likely the following day, as this was a Sunday, that a rather surprised visitor arrived in Tideswell, fully expecting the village to be its usual self. This visitor was none other than John Longden, a popular and much respected Methodist preacher, who had walked all the way to Tideswell from his home with the intention of morally stirring his congregation to great things. He would later become landlord of the Snake Pass Inn within the Snake Pass itself, which much to his delight brought him into contact with many of his fellow human beings. Seeing the chance to get across his beliefs, he also used the inn as a place of worship and often held prayer meetings there so that he could indeed spread his preachings.

However, much to his astonishment, on this day the place of worship he was to preach at was devoid of a good deal of its congregation, a most unusual happening considering that his popularity often drew a full house. When he enquired where his flock had gone he was told in no uncertain terms as to their whereabouts. Not being one to miss an opportunity, Longden immediately set off to the gibbet site and would undoubtedly have been aghast at the vision that met him. The fair-like atmosphere with the stalls and pedlars, along with the hoards of tourists all milling around and enjoying the day, topped off by the macabre sight of Lingard's body hanging high above their heads, would undoubtedly have stirred the religious fervour inside Longden. Without further ado, he proceeded to the gibbet post and began to deliver a sermon that was both rousing and delivered with feeling, for this was the kind of pulpit that preachers of the likes of Longden could use to their best advantage. Had it not been for such a serious and important matter then the whole scene could have been described as comical, with hawkers and traders all trying to sell their wares to tourists and locals alike, pickpockets and con men milling with the crowd and trying to make an illegal shilling or two, and John Longden loudly espousing his beliefs to all that would listen, while all this time the remains of Anthony Lingard were swaying in the breeze above their heads.

The cost of a life can at times be cheap, as in the case of Hannah Oliver, whose life was worth a new pair of red shoes and a few pounds, but by contrast the price of a death can be very expensive. In the case of Anthony Lingard we know the costs of his arrest and death almost down to the last penny, where the expense for his being apprehended was £31 5s 5d (£31.27p), the charges made by the gaoler for the transportation of the body from Derby to Wardlow Mires were £10 10s (£10.50p) and the cost of the gibbeting being the huge sum of £85 4s 1d (£85.20p); this cost included the 16 shillings paid to each of the three constables for their two days' work in policing the gibbeting. In short, the total cost of justice being seen to be done was a few pence under £127, and two lives.

# HANNAH BOCKING

The use of gibbeting was justified as being a deterrent to other would-be criminals, who, it was thought, would see the consequences of taking to a life of crime and decide against it. It is sad to say that not many heeded these warnings and continued down the path that would ultimately lead to their own death. Not all those that took to this path had any choice, however, sometimes they were driven to it by sheer hunger or the threat of starvation.

While Lingard had been languishing in gaol awaiting his trial Napoleon had made his escape from Elba and was busily recreating his power base in Europe. Once again the British government was in confusion as, after believing that it had solved the problem of France and Napoleon once and for all, it now found itself in an even worse position. The short respite of Napoleon's imprisonment had led to the belief that the country could start to get back to something like normality. For decades the economy had been on a war footing and the whole of the country needed a period of stable peace. Yet again, the ruling classes started to look over their shoulders (not that they had ever stopped) to seek out revolutionaries in their own back yard, as well as threats from abroad. The long years of war had not been bad news for everyone, however. The industrialists and the industrial working class in the towns and cities had done quite well out of it as the production of goods for the war effort had rocketed, but, although the wages for workers in towns had risen steadily, their lives were shortened by squalid living conditions and harsh working practices. However, it was life in the countryside that bore the brunt of the economic troubles. Wages were almost stagnant yet prices kept on rising, and unless the government acted quickly then something would give.

In June 1815 the Duke of Wellington confronted Napoleon and his army at Waterloo and managed once and for all to defeat the French. Peace did not bring about the much sought-after revival in fortunes for the government, though, as the demobilised army and navy flooded the labour market with the unemployed and the unemployable. A great number of those that had joined the forces had been convicted criminals, who had been given the choice of gaol or military service, while some had joined just to escape justice and were now free to once again take up their old careers. The year passed by and still taxation was high; food prices remained high and jobs were hard to come by. The New Year came and with it more disaster, for as spring came and went it was obvious that the crops were not doing as well as they should be, and 1816 in fact became known as 'the year with no summer'. In April 1815 the volcano Mount Tambora on the island of Sumbawa in Indonesia had erupted with such violence that the ash and smoke it threw into the atmosphere caused a change in the climate. Throughout Europe it has been estimated that over 200,000 people died from starvation and an epidemic of typhus that were a direct result of this cataclysmic explosion. In France and Switzerland there were food riots, while in Britain the shortage of food caused prices to rise once again. Inflation started to get out of control and it stayed that way for the next three or four years. In London there were riots over the way the people were being repressed, and this was just the tip of the iceberg.

The year 1817 saw the harvest fail once again, which led to more misery, and *habeas corpus* was suspended by the government: in other words the basic right to justice was taken away. In this same year a group of cotton workers planned to march from Manchester to London in protest against the loss of income, but this too was seen as a threat by the government of Lord Liverpool and it was broken up. Manchester is a little over 30 miles from Litton and Tideswell and the repercussions of all these actions would have filtered through to everyone in the area and more than likely would have thrown doubt and worry into their already troubled lives. In the East Midlands, workers broke up machinery in order to safeguard their jobs, only to find that their ranks were being infiltrated by government spies. So paranoid were the ruling classes about insurrection and revolution that they used spies to stir up and even invent trouble just so the alleged ringleaders could be isolated and dealt with in apparent open and transparent justice. Not everyone was fooled by this strategy, though, and it created an even deeper-seated hatred among those that clamoured for change. The common man and woman knew very little of all these manoeuvrings, yet they were the ones that bore the brunt of all the political fallout, and to survive some of them had to use their wits or go under.

All the time that this was going on the gibbet at Wardlow Mires stood tall and erect with Lingard's corpse still on view for all to see and hopefully to deter the desperate or the greedy from entering a life of crime. The question was, would it actually work? Many travellers making their way along the toll road would look across and see this grizzly sight and probably wonder what had caused such a quiet backwater as this to be branded with such infamy. In 1818 Ebenezer Rhodes published a book entitled *Peak Scenery* in which he described his earlier travels around Derbyshire and its area. In it he recalls how he came across the sight of Lingard, and his simple but plain speaking words sum up his thoughts on the matter:

*'One would suppose that there was but little on these bleak hills and plains to excite the cupidity of the robber, or to induce the commission of the crime of murder, particularly among a people whose wants are necessarily as circumscribed as their means; but even here, at a little distance on the left of the road, we observed a man suspended on a gibbet, but newly erected. He had entered the cottage of a poor woman who kept the toll gate at Wardlow-Mears, [sic] and this for the paltry consideration of a few shillings.'*

The spring and summer of that year passed much the same as all the other seasons had done, food was still at a premium for some as once again the harvest had been poor and shortages were not uncommon. It was important to find and keep employment so that it gave another source of income for all the family to share and it was this consideration that was foremost in the mind of another resident of Litton, Hannah Bocking. Sixteen-year-old Hannah was regarded as having a strange and bad type of personality that could manifest itself into violent acts, yet as August became September she surprisingly became friends with a young woman by the name of Jane Grant. It was regarded as surprising because the 21-year-old Jane had actually been given Hannah's job within the household of the Brammer family, also of Litton, after she had been dismissed for her poor attitude and more importantly because of her distinctly bad temperament and disposition. Yet Hannah's advances of friendship towards Jane were strangely enough accepted, perhaps Jane had a kindly nature and felt sorry for the younger girl, or it might have been that she was frightened of Hannah and felt that to reject her overtures of friendship might lead to some kind of reprisal, possibly even violence. No matter how Hannah's disposition was described, there is evidence to show that she was not an unintelligent young woman. It is known that she could read and this alone could stand her apart from quite a large portion of the population, who never had the opportunity to learn any academic skills, and regardless of her obviously foul temperament she did indeed have a number of real friends and was loved by her family. Perhaps it is not so surprising, then, that Jane Grant started to become friends with Hannah, especially if Hannah was intelligent enough to be able to manipulate people and situations for her own benefit.

One day in the early part of September the two young women were walking to the fields near Wardlow to let out and tend to some cattle close to the gibbet where the corpse of Anthony Lingard still hung. When they were close to the gibbet Hannah gave Jane a gift. To show the friendship that had blossomed between them, Hannah had baked a cake and now she presented it to Jane. It is not known if Jane ate the cake there and then or saved it for later, but it is a fact that she ate some or all of it at one point for soon she became ill. Unbeknown to Jane, the cake she had eaten was laced with arsenic; Hannah was showing her true colours at last. For the amount of arsenic that Jane had consumed the first symptoms would have come after about half an hour, giving her ample time to make her way home, even when the initial signs manifested themselves. To start with she would have had a metallic taste in her mouth, she would be producing excessive amounts of saliva and have difficulty swallowing, then she would start vomiting and have uncontrollable diarrhoea, followed by excruciating stomach cramps and profuse sweating. Those around her would smell a garlic-like odour on her breath and not once would anyone have guessed what was wrong with her. All the cures and remedies were useless, for even had they known the cause of her agonising throes it was already too late to save her. Soon she would begin to have seizures, would go into shock and thankfully fall into a coma, her internal organs would then begin to fail and finally death would be the only possible outcome. Jane's widowed mother, also called Jane, would have had no chance to help her daughter, as from the moment she bit into that sweet cake all chance of survival had gone. If she was lucky, the concentration of arsenic would have been such that death would have occurred within just a few short hours, but if, however, she had had less than the full dose it is possible she would have lingered on for many hours indeed. It is hard to imagine what Jane Grant the elder was going through at that time, for Jane was the second grown-up daughter that she had lost in the last three and a half years. Her other daughter Sarah had died at the age of 28, just after the murder of Hannah Oliver, and so this double tragedy was without any doubt a devastating blow for her.

Word soon spread about the happenings at the home of the Grants and it did not take very long for the real reason for the younger Jane's death to become apparent, nor was it long before suspicions began to be raised about Hannah Bocking's involvement. Hannah was questioned by the authorities but staunchly denied any involvement, yet such was the weight of belief in her guilt that she was arrested and taken to the gaol in Derby, the very same gaol that her fellow citizen of Litton, Anthony Lingard, had been taken to less than four years previously. On 19 September 1818 Hannah Bocking was committed to the gaol by the coroner James Mander and, ironically, on that very same day in Tideswell, Jane Grant the elder laid her beloved daughter to rest. The entry in the parish records was amended at a later date to include the words:

*'Poisoned wilfully by arsenic by Hannah Bocking who was executed at Derby 22 March 1819'*

Such simple words hiding so much pain.

While in the gaol, Hannah would have walked where Lingard would have walked, she could possibly have slept in the same cell that Lingard had slept in, and she would have eaten the same type of food and suffered the same cramped, stinking, smelly conditions that Lingard had endured, and all the time she was locked up awaiting trial she denied her guilt. She went as far as to implicate others for perpetrating the foul deed and pointed the finger of blame at a number of her relatives, including, at one time, her own sister. This younger sister was described in the *Derby Mercury* as being '…of delicate health…' and the accusations made against her caused her to suffer dreadfully.

For six months Hannah Bocking was kept incarcerated in Derby gaol awaiting her trial, until at last the March assizes of 1819 came around, with the ritual ceremony taking place once again upon the arrival of the assizes judge, the Honourable Sir James Burrough. As always, there was the pre-assizes sermon given in the All Saints Church by the Revd Anson this time, with the stirring theme of 'Righteousness exalteth a nation: but sin is a reproach to any people'. The question is, just who was he trying to convert? From the subjects of his sermons it seems he was trying to tell those assembled that whatever sentence they passed in the coming days they were justified by his interpretation of the Bible. Perhaps this was what he meant, but yet again perhaps it was not.

The assizes were convened and one by one the cases were heard, with the judge solemnly passing the death sentence on many occasions, until at last it came to Hannah Bocking, the small 16-year-old girl from Litton, a little country village in the hills of Derbyshire.

As the trial began to take shape and the evidence started to mount against her, those inside the courtroom noticed with some disquiet that Hannah seemed to be dispassionate about the whole proceedings and, in fact, treated them with a marked lack of emotion, even though those around her found the case distinctly distressing. They could not understand how one so young could commit such a foul deed and remain so totally unmoved or so deeply unrepentant. All the time she had spent in the gaol awaiting her time in court she had portrayed the same attitude, one of complete disinterest, it was almost as if she had resigned herself to her fate and in some respects had expected it from the outset.

The proof against Hannah was steadily building, yet her fate was sealed when it was shown that she had bought the poison at least 10 weeks before it had been used in the cake. This was no spur-of-the-moment revenge attack, this was a premeditated, deliberate murder that had taken time to arrange and execute. With such strong evidence against her, coupled with her own attitude towards her predicament, the jury could only come to one verdict, even for one so young. As in the case of Anthony Lingard, the judge donned his black cap and passed the sentence of death by hanging, with the addition that her body be afterwards 'anatomised and dissected'. Once more the members of the public and reporters within the courtroom noticed a distinct lack of concern on Hannah's part, even as the sentence was passed.

With the trial concluded, Hannah was taken from the Shire Hall back to the gaol on Friargate, where she was allowed to receive a visit from some of her friends, who, after all that had been done and said, still thought of her that way. No one will ever know what was said during that visit, but it did have an effect on her for her attitude softened and she became more aware of the dire situation she was in. Despite this it is on record that the night before her execution Hannah slept soundly, appearing quite unperturbed at the prospects of her forthcoming death, yet she too would have heard the same sounds as Lingard did as the workmen busied themselves in preparing the execution scaffold that would soon be used.

For one so young to commit such a crime seemed unreal to many people, and before Hannah was led to the scaffold she had a number of visitors. The Revd Pickering, the chaplain of the gaol, came to perform his religious duties, as did a Methodist minister, which implies that Hannah had been brought up in that denomination, and several ladies, who expressed concern as to Hannah's fate. As the time drew near for her execution she spent time in the chapel of the gaol and it was while she was there that she was seen by Thomas Hopkinson, a young man of about 20 years, who had just returned to the gaol from the Shire Hall after having had the death sentence passed on him for highway robbery. He knew that within the hour Hannah would be dead and that his time would come within days, if not hours.

At the appointed hour Hannah's arms were bound by her sides, leaving her hands free, and she was led to the scaffold in front of the gaol and there she took a few words of comfort from the chaplain before the hood was pulled over her face and she was sent to her death. Most people think that the hood is there to hide the scaffold from the condemned and make their ending more humane but this is not so; the hood is there to protect the crowd from seeing the contorted face of the prisoner as they go through the death throes and to stop them being showered with any blood that might be sprayed around as blood vessels burst and the prisoner fights to live. If it had been intended to protect the sensibilities of the prisoners then the hood would be fitted before they saw the scaffold.

On that fine and calm March day a huge crowd watched as the first woman in over 60 years was executed in Derby and they gave what was later described as 'an involuntary shuddering' at what they had seen. Perhaps it was a last-minute pang of remorse or perhaps she thought it the right time to perform one last good deed, but before Hannah was sent to her death she retracted all the accusations she had made against others for the murder of Jane Grant and acknowledged her own guilt, yet it is likely that the damage had already been done to those innocent reputations.

After hanging for the usual time (until the authorities were reasonably sure that Hannah was dead), her body was cut down and taken back to the Shire Hall for dissection. The pleas from friends and relatives to have her body released to them so that they might give her a decent burial was denied and a rather macabre procession made its way back to St Mary's Gate in readiness for the surgeons to do their work. Once inside the Shire Hall, her body was placed in such a position that the dissection could take place with as many spectators as possible. Medical men would be eager to get an insight into how the body worked and to have such a fresh specimen to work on was indeed a pleasant change. Members of the local gentry would also try to get in to view the proceedings, for they too might find it of interest, and, lastly, if there was any room left, then members of the public would be given admittance. For those that could not get inside the hall then all was not lost because once the cutting and carving of the cadaver had taken place and the questions of those inside had been answered as to the workings of the human body, all of Hannah's body parts, her internal organs and her cut-up body were put on public display. Here the parts would remain for two or three days while the general public filed past to view this horrific sight, which also served the purpose of proving that justice had been done. When curiosity had faded away and the pieces of flesh started to go off they were disposed of, not in a formal grave but usually just discarded. In some cases, parts were kept for medical study or just out of plain interest and placed on display; in Hannah's case it seems that nothing has been kept, so in effect she has just disappeared.

At the March assizes of 1819 the death sentence was passed 19 times but out of those only two were executed while the rest had their sentences commuted to varying lengths of transportation. Hannah Bocking was a murderess and so perhaps fully deserved the penalty of the law, yet Thomas Hopkinson was not. He was convicted of a highway robbery in which no one was killed. It is true that he was a long-term troublemaker and was the perpetrator of many crimes[4], but did he deserve to hang? Times were changing, not only for those who were trying to make an honest living but also for those who were convicted of crimes, whether justly or not.

# WITHIN SIGHT OF THE GIBBET

When Thomas Hopkinson met his death a few days after Hannah Bocking it was perhaps ironic that he had come to this point because his partner in crime, John Fletcher, had turned King's evidence in order to save his own life and it was this exact same course of action that Hopkinson had taken two years earlier. He had given evidence to the court that had convicted four of his accomplices of the crime of setting fire to haystacks while he himself walked free, and so when Hopkinson stood on the gallows awaiting the drop one man was watching intently. One of Hopkinson's accomplices in the firing of the haystacks was Thomas Jackson, and at his execution Jackson's estranged father had witnessed his son's last moments, so when it became knowledge that Hopkinson too was to be put to death Jackson's father applied for the job of hangman. Whether it was because the position had already been filled or whether it was because the authorities deemed it not appropriate for such a person to perform the executioner's duties is not known, but it is perhaps fortunate for Hopkinson that Jackson did not get the job.

This was the type of society that was being bred throughout the country, one of suspicion, hate and mistrust, where crime could pay if the criminal was clever enough to evade identification and capture. Life was cheap and, as it is often said, it always had been, yet the climate of war that had existed for decades had taught generations of young men and women to fight for everything, otherwise what they believed was rightly theirs would be taken away.

The raging inflation continued right up to the 1820s, with just a small respite of about a year when there was a small economic boom that lessened the hardships and gave false hope to a weary nation. In 1819 the government was left reeling when a crowd of up to 80,000 made their way to listen to Henry 'Orator' Hunt speak at St Peter's Fields in Manchester and the local magistrates, fearing disorder, ordered the cavalry to charge. The resultant carnage became known as the Peterloo Massacre and it left 11 dead, scores injured and authority in disrepute. While Hunt was arrested, another of the main speakers, Richard Carlile, managed to escape and after being hidden by friends was able to avoid the clutches of the magistrates by fleeing to London on the mail coach. Once again, with Manchester being relatively close to Litton and the surrounding area, the fallout would have had a profound effect. Inwardly, the government was appalled but they needed to show that the rule of law had to be upheld, so publicly the actions were commended. The following year proved to be memorable for different reasons: King George III died and one of the last major conspiracies to overthrow a British government took place. The Cato Street Plot was designed to kill the entire cabinet – not quite the same as the failed Pentrich Rebellion, which had been a group of disaffected men from Derbyshire, who had a wild plan to take action using popular support – but a more serious attempt to change the course of British politics by murder. The probability is that both of these actions were set up by government agents just to give agitators a focus that could be controlled. Indeed, the Pentrich Rebellion had been influenced by the government spy known as 'Oliver'. Rather ironically, the country was being ruled by one of the strongest cabinets ever and its policies would eventually reap benefits, but the process was taking time and the hungry and deprived people lacked patience.

Trade began to revive as exports started to rise in the post-war era, but one of the main problems stemmed from the Corn Laws that kept the price of bread artificially high. In rural areas, such as those around Litton and Tideswell where there was also industry, villages and towns seemed to be becoming polarised between those that were doing relatively well because of a rise in exports and the resultant influx in money and those that relied on agriculture. The subsidies that landowners were receiving annoyed and angered many of those that saw this as an unfair advantage and a lot of those employed at the sharp end of agriculture went bankrupt. The mills at Cressbrook and Litton would have been hard places to work in with their tough working environments but at least the workers had money in their pockets to buy food, whereas the farmer and agricultural worker very often found themselves on the breadline. The year 1821 saw the beginning of a famine in Ireland that would last for three years, so by comparison the population in England were doing better than they thought. In 1825 a landmark was reached when trade unions were legalised, yet still the area where Lingard and Bocking had come from was regarded as being bleak and inhospitable. It was a poor area to live in because of the hardships of survival for the majority.

Whenever and wherever there is hardship it can be guaranteed that there will be someone who can find a way to make quick money, either from those that already have little but are gullible, or from those that have had good fortune and have managed to make some money but fail to keep it safe and sound. In the 19th century, travel was becoming safer than it had been in previous years but it was still not advisable to travel alone or at night in lonely or secluded spots. The heyday of the highwayman and footpad was pretty much a faded memory because of the improving network of roads and the efforts of the authorities to foster a safer environment, yet it was still dangerous to travel unprepared. Sometimes it was complacency and sometimes naivety that allowed travellers to take fewer precautions than were needed.

The years had passed slowly since Hannah Bocking and Anthony Lingard had met the executioner and for a while the inhabitants of Litton, Tideswell, Wardlow and all the surrounding villages had been lulled into a false sense of security. Lingard's rotting corpse still swung on the gibbet as a warning to all visitors of the dangers of transgressing the laws of the land, even though in the case of Hannah Bocking it had no effect. Perhaps this stark warning did have an effect on some who saw it, yet equally it had the reverse effect on some.

By July 1825 business was picking up and John Bagshaw, a butcher from Great Hucklow, a small village just a short distance from Litton and Wardlow, had decided to attend the market being held in Litton on 30 July so that he could sell some of his products. The day must have gone well for as he rode his Galloway, a stocky, strong breed of horse ideal as a beast of burden, on the way to his home he decided to stop at an inn to refresh himself. While at the public house he noticed that he had company in the guise of two young men, one of whom was William Lingard, younger brother to Anthony, the executed murderer whose rotting body hung in chains nearby. William Lingard's pale blue eyes watched Bagshaw take his refreshments as thoughts began to go through his head. Lingard, who was a little over 5ft 6in tall with brown hair and a sallow complexion, could have hidden his strength built up from a life of labouring beneath his rough clothing. As a weaver, life would not have been as hard as that of a farm labourer but still the continual toil would have built up his physique. The days of the frame-work knitter were virtually over so in all probability Lingard was a worker from either the mill at Cressbrook or more probably the infamous Litton Mill. His wife, Ann, had given birth to their daughter Hannah just over four months before and with an extra mouth to feed the pressure to bring in an extra income to supplement what little they had would have been great.

Lingard's companion was William Bennett, another local man who had already tried his hand at being a petty criminal. Perhaps his previous experiences had given him a false sense of security because just the preceding November he had been arrested for highway robbery and acquitted. At the following Derby assizes the evidence against him was possibly circumspect for he was 'discharged by proclamation', a term used for being found not guilty or being released without punishment. It was claimed that Bennett had assaulted George Dakin on the turnpike road from Chesterfield as it neared Tideswell and had taken from him three pound notes that had been issued by the Wirksworth Bank, two pound notes from the Macclesfield Bank and some silver. With his trial over and Bennett freed, he returned to his old haunt and took up his life once again. Within months he would try his hand at highway robbery once more.

Bagshaw was presumably unaware of his fellow drinkers' thoughts and so, with a false sense of security, he finished his refreshments and made his way back to his horse. Remounting the Galloway, he turned and continued on his way home, deciding, probably through necessity, to travel alone rather than seek a companion. It was always advisable to seek trustworthy company when using the highways and byways to help lessen the chance of robbery, especially when carrying money or valuables as Bagshaw appeared to be. As he began his way home a woman by the name of Fanny Ryals was standing opposite the inn, and even though the hour was late she saw one of the young men coming out of the public house and make his way into a back yard. Bagshaw was making his way home using a route that took him through an area known as Denston Bottom and the shortest way to this place from the inn was to exit by using the back yard as described by Fanny Ryals.

As Bagshaw reached Denston Bottom, barely a mile from the inn, he noticed the two young men he had seen earlier hiding in some nettles, one on each side of the road. He realised too late that he was in danger and before he could defend himself or turn and flee William Lingard had leapt up and pulled him from his horse and was forcibly holding him down. Fearing for what might be done if he resisted he cried out, 'Lads, don't use me ill, I am an old man, and if you'll give me time, I'll give you my money'.

As Bagshaw lay pinned to the ground, William Bennett reached out and took his purse and pocket book, which in total netted the robbers one pound note and one guinea note (£1.05p), a virtual fortune to those who had little or nothing. With their task complete, the robbers made good their escape without really realising the gravity of the act they had committed, for they were now wanted criminals or, to be more precise, wanted highwaymen, a crime still regarded as one of the most serious of all.

Their good luck did not last for long, however, for within hours William Bennett had been captured and was sent unceremoniously to await his fate at Derby gaol and on 1 August, just two days after perpetrating the crime, Messrs Shuttleworth and Middleton committed Bennett to the infamous gaol on Friargate. All records of what Bennett thought or said while in gaol have been lost but it is easy to imagine that this 21-year-old must have bemoaned all that had befallen him, especially if the original idea for the robbery had not been his. He did not have to worry about carrying the burden of the crime on his own shoulders for long, if that is indeed what happened, for just three days later on 4 August his accomplice was also committed to the gaol by Shuttleworth and Middleton. This time an eyebrow or two would have been raised, especially by those with long memories, for the 19-year-old man who was arrested for the highway robbery of John Bagshaw along with William Bennett was William Lingard, the younger brother of the executed Anthony Lingard.

Was it desperation, bravado or drunkenness that led to the crime? Perhaps it was none of these, but nevertheless the example that had been set by the execution of Anthony Lingard had had no effect on his sibling, for the ambush and robbery of John Bagshaw had taken place within sight of the rotting and decaying corpse of the gibbeted Lingard. Neither the fear of capture after the crime nor the constant sight of his brother's parched bones over the years had done anything to dissuade William Lingard from a course of crime, so was it really a deterrent to gibbet the body of executed prisoners? Just who had been the instigator of the highway robbery was never disclosed but in the eyes of the law both of them were equally responsible.

Bennett and Lingard were kept locked within the walls of the gaol until the March assizes of 1826. More than seven months passed until it was their time to stand trial for their lives and in all that time they had slept where Anthony Lingard had slept, they had eaten where Anthony Lingard had eaten and they had walked and talked where Anthony Lingard had done so. It is more than likely that it had no effect on the younger Lingard but it made Bennett realise the situation they were in. Future events would show their true personalities and traits but for now they were accused prisoners who were about to go on trial for their lives, and they would surely have been made aware of the fate of other highway robbers such as Thomas Hopkinson.

The assizes were opened by a resplendent Sir Joseph Littledale, a man who, like all his colleagues, believed in the righteousness of the law and that it should be upheld. One by one he heard the cases, passing judgements as he deemed fit for those found guilty, until it was time for Lingard and Bennett to take their places in the dock. Perhaps thinking that honesty was the best policy and hoping for a reduced sentence, Bennett entered a plea of guilty. Lingard, it would seem, decided to challenge his accusers and after his main accuser John Bagshaw had given his evidence he was asked if he wished to put questions to him. Lingard's question was a simple one and probably his only hope of acquittal as well: had his accuser not said that he was unsure that Lingard was one of those that had robbed him? The question was a simple one indeed and so was the answer, for Bagshaw denied ever saying those words. With the testimonies of John Bagshaw and Fanny Ryals, who recounted her story of seeing Lingard enter the yard, the trial was, for all intents and purposes, over and Bennett and Lingard had to be prepared for whatever might come. The guilty verdict was a foregone conclusion as the evidence was overwhelming and so Judge Littledale passed the usual sentence of death on the two accomplices. It was indeed fortunate for the two prisoners that there had been a general change in attitude towards the overuse of capital punishment because before the judge left Derby to continue his work elsewhere he commuted both of their sentences to that of transportation for life. The length of transportation sentences fell into three categories: seven years, 14 years and life, with life usually meaning for the whole life of the convict – even if granted a pardon it was very rare for the newly freed convict to be allowed to return to his native country.

There were three destinations to which transported prisoners could be sent after serving a part of their sentence in this country on-board a hulk ship. A hulk ship was a privately run prison ship, which was usually de-masted and converted to hold convicts. Conditions were often appalling and if the convicts survived relatively unscathed they would be sent to either the West Indies, Gibraltar or Australia to finish off their sentence. Those sent to the West Indies faced the prospect of tropical disease, being treated as almost slave labour on plantations and possibly an early death, while those going to Gibraltar had to look forward to incarceration on hulk ships that would have been terrible places to spend months and years in, with squalid and filthy conditions to also contend with.

Those who were deemed fortunate enough to be sent to Australia stood the chance of a more comfortable outlook, with a life in a new country and the possibility of limited freedom. It is a myth that all convicts were sent to Botany Bay as this was an unsuitable piece of coastline; the real destination for many of the convict ships was across the bay to an area that is now part of the Sydney area of Australia. It is inconceivable that Bennett and Lingard had any idea what or where Australia and the other possible destinations even were, let alone the type of life that was facing them. The term transportation was something that they would have heard of but could in no way have understood what it actually represented. In reality it was the taking away of a complete way of life, and the family that they had grown up with would remain just a distant memory. Everything familiar would be removed from their life, and for those that managed to escape and make their way back to the country of their birth, execution would be guaranteed if caught.

Bennett and Lingard were returned to Friargate and placed back in the cells to wait while all the necessary arrangements were made to take them to one of the hulk ships, which would hold them until a suitable transport ship was available to take them on their one-way trip away from these shores.

Back in Wardlow Mires and Litton, things were also happening to change the future and eradicate the past from the immediate area. There had been many complaints about the gibbet and the disturbing sound that Anthony Lingard's bones were making as they rattled against the metal frame in which they had been kept for 11 years. Locals said that as the breeze and winds blew the noise was so disturbing that they were kept awake and that the constant stream of sightseers was causing disruption to their lives, so a petition was made to the magistrates to have the gibbet and remains removed. Thankfully for those concerned, their wish was granted and on 10 or 11 April 1826, just over 11 years after it was erected, the gibbet was pulled down, with most of Lingard's bones being buried in the ground beneath the site of the gibbet post itself.

The warning message intended to be given out by the gibbeting of Anthony Lingard had not worked and his younger brother, who sat in jail at the same time as his brother's remains were being interred, was proof of this. For nearly a month Bennett and Lingard were kept in gaol until it was time for their departure to begin an unknown life. For those left behind, the only reference of their departure appeared in the *Derby Mercury* on 3 May, when one small passage announced the fate of all the convicted prisoners of Derby:

*'On Saturday last, the undermentioned convicts were removed from the county gaol to the Justicia [sic] Hulk lying of Woolwich, where they will remain until their several sentences of transportation can be further carried into effect; viz Thomas and William Hardy for seven years; and William Lingard for life. Yesterday the following convicts were removed from the said prison for the same destination, viz. William Bennett for life, John Slack, John Rowland alias Gibson and William Bower alias Hopkins, for seven years.'*

# EXILE

**W**ithin days Lingard and Bennett had made the difficult and uncomfortable journey all the way down to Woolwich on the River Thames, where they were to spend a potentially unlimited time until a convict transporter arrived to take them to the other side of the world. Initially, all the newly arrived convicts were taken to a nearby hospital ship to make sure that they had not brought any illness or disease with them, which if they had could have caused an outbreak on-board that would have been almost uncontrollable in such cramped and appallingly filthy conditions. One of the first things that would have happened is that all the prisoners would have had their clothes taken away from them and prison issue ones given in their place. The prisoners' old clothes would be cleaned, mended and given to those that had completed their sentences and were due for release. After what was viewed as a suitable time, Bennett, Lingard and the new convicts were transferred to the *Justitia*, a ship normally described as an old East Indiaman, which meant that it was an old cargo ship pressed into service as a prison ship after undergoing a hasty and usually unsuitable conversion. While on-board the *Justitia* life for all the prisoners was hard. They worked, ate and slept in irons, with idleness being punished by being double ironed. Those that were fit enough were set to work on Woolwich docks, while those deemed below par were kept on-board and had to spend the day either doing menial tasks or nothing at all. It was thought preferable to work ashore for this brought a relief from the awful conditions on-board ship and also gave the chance for the convicts to trade and barter with the free workers that they encountered.

One former convict, William Derricourt, wrote of his time on the *Justitia* and his words manage to convey some of the hardships that had to be endured. In total, there were three ships called *Justitia*. Bennett and Lingard were on the second vessel given this name, while Derricourt was on the third, yet conditions would have been very similar for Derricourt's experiences started only about four or five years after Bennett and Lingard arrived.

Derricourt tells us that on arrival at the hospital ship he was completely stripped. He was scrubbed with soap and a hard brush until his skin bled and his hair was cut so close as to be almost shaved off. He was then given his prison clothes before being taken to the blacksmith, who riveted on iron ankle rings which were connected by eight links to a central ring. This ring was in turn fastened by a strap or cord to a belt around the waist so as to stop the ankle chains from trailing on the ground; he then had straps put around his knees so that the chains could be fastened to them, allowing their weight to be passed to his calves. At long last he was transferred to the *Justitia* and hoped that he would never have to set foot on the hospital ships again, for conditions on-board were deplorable and medical provision was minimal and basic. On the *Justitia*, too, conditions were dire, with the low decks meaning it was impossible to stand upright, while all forms of openings on the landward side were covered over to restrict the chance of escape. At night time the prisoners were locked below decks, which left the more vulnerable open to abuse and persecution by the stronger and more violent criminals. It was not unknown for a weaker prisoner to meet his death at the hands of one of his fellow inmates and quite often the guards did little to prevent it happening, only taking action when it was too late, for many of them thought it was too dangerous to go below deck alone after dark.

Some years earlier in 1809, on-board one of the hulks moored at Woolwich, 20-year-old William Colman for some unknown reason threw an object (described as a brick) at one of the guards. Although the guard did not see the perpetrator of the act, suspicion fell upon Colman. Knowing that he had not been seen by the guard, he suspected that a fellow prisoner by the name of Thomas Jones had informed on him. Colman repeatedly swore revenge on Jones but, remarkably, within a short time the rift appeared to have been patched up when both convicts shook hands and had a drink together. With the trouble behind them, Jones helped Colman into his bed, a task that Colman found difficult to do on his own because he was heavily laden with irons. Colman lay in his bed for quite some time pretending to be asleep and when he supposed that all those around him were slumbering he quietly rose and went to a secret hiding place where he knew there was a knife. Careful not to make any noise, he made his way to where Jones was asleep and deliberately and without hesitation stabbed him in the neck and chest time after time. Jones died instantly. Colman had not been careful enough in his endeavours to be quiet, however, and two fellow convicts had seen the whole episode. Many of those on the hulks were men and women who had committed very minor crimes so an act such as this would stir up a sense of duty and compel them to tell all they knew to the authorities. In other cases it was well known that should a convict help in such a serious matter their time on-board these terrible ships could be made more comfortable or possibly reduced. Whatever the reasoning, the two convicts that had seen Colman's actions stood in the witness box and gave the damning evidence that condemned Colman to be hanged. Such was life on the hulks that no one's safety was guaranteed.

With the hatches closed at nights and most of the other openings sealed off permanently, the air would be rancid and foul as the smell of scores of unwashed bodies mixed with the stench coming from the stagnant water in the bilges. This was the sort of life that Bennett and Lingard had to look forward to for the foreseeable future until their departure for Australia.

Those who were fit enough had the task of working on engineering projects at the Woolwich Arsenal and docks. This was treated as a way of keeping the convicts active, helped to suppress frustrations and anger, and at the same time provided cheap labour for government projects. On the hulks the prisoners would watch for any ships passing by that might have soldiers on-board, for this would mean that it was a convict ship and transportation could be imminent, and if any of them died in the meantime their bodies would be rowed down stream and buried in a specially designated area on the river bank with no headstone or grave marker to show their final resting place. For those that were sentenced to seven years' transportation there was some hope, for they were allowed to work hard, and if they kept out of trouble they could qualify for a pardon. This gave some of them something to aim for, but for those sentenced to 14 years or life no such incentive existed. These convicts, both men and women, had to serve their sentences out in foreign parts.

The drudgery of hulk ship life went on until early August when Bennett, Lingard and many of their fellow prisoners were sent further down the Thames to Sheerness, where they were taken aboard the convict ship *Speke*, an old ship of just 473 tons that had been built in 1790 in Calcutta. This old cargo ship had been converted to take a different kind of cargo – a human cargo. Very often these older ships were inadequate for this purpose, with the height between the decks being low as the shipyard and vessel owners did their best to create room for as many prisoners as possible. The more convicts that could be carried then the more revenue they could generate on each voyage, and that was one of the major dictates for these privately run ships. Now, after a little over three months at Woolwich, Bennett and Lingard were finally leaving the country of their birth – never to return. Some convicts treated transportation as the chance of a new life and a new beginning, while others saw it as the time when they lost everything that made life worthwhile.

On 8 August 1826, Bennett, Lingard and 154 other male convicts set sail on the *Speke* chained up in the cramped conditions below decks. During the long trips of transportation the health and welfare of the convicts was entrusted to the ship's superintendent surgeon, who had authority over the ship's captain in matters concerning the prisoners. In Bennett and Lingard's case they were fortunate that the superintendent surgeon on the *Speke* was Alick Osborne, a man who would make a total of 10 trips aboard convict ships in that capacity and gain a great reputation for being an able and caring doctor. Robert Harrison was the ship's master, and although little is known about him, we do know that this was one of only two trips he would make in that capacity. His second trip in charge was as master of the *Guildford,* which set sail from Dublin in April 1829, its long voyage claiming the lives of four convicts. Considering Harrison and Osborne's success in delivering all the prisoners on-board the *Speke* alive to their destination, it says much for their skill.

The months at sea would have been awful for those that suffered from seasickness, bearing in mind that many of those on the ship had never even seen the ocean before never mind been on a ship. Yet it was the duty of the surgeon to keep the convicts healthy, not only in mind but also in body. If the prisoners took ill then he tended their needs and administered medication as needed, all the time keeping meticulous records. (There are many recorded cases where the efforts of the surgeons saved the lives of sick prisoners and stopped the illness spreading.) Not only did they act as ship's doctor, but they also gave advice on the food that was to be served up and would draw up a menu that the cook had to prepare. Yet even this was not the end of their duties as they also had to tend to the spiritual and intellectual needs of those confined on-board. The surgeon had to draw up a timetable for every day of the week in which each hour of the day had a task for the prisoners to perform, ranging from times allocated for meals or exercise on deck, to religious instruction and educational lessons where they learnt to read and write. For those willing to commit some effort into their time on the ships it could be of benefit for them when they arrived in Australia. These regimes not only helped to improve the minds of a lot of the convicts but also helped to maintain discipline while at sea and thus make the trip less arduous. In the early days of transportation there was no provision for medical or humanitarian welfare for the convicts in any form. The captain of the ship had just one duty and that was to make sure he delivered his cargo to its destination in the shortest time possible. There were many deaths on the early voyages because of the poor conditions and even poorer food, with some of the captains deliberately failing to stop at the usual re-provisioning ports, such as Cape Town, so that the journey could be completed more quickly. It was only after much deliberation that it was decided to create the new post of superintendant surgeon. The surgeon's job was regarded as so important that the captain had to obey him in all matters concerning the prisoners' welfare, with the captain only retaining jurisdiction over the safety of the ship.

After 110 days at sea the *Speke* finally arrived at its destination in Australia and reached the area near Sydney, New South Wales, on 26 November, making it the fastest crossing in nearly two years and with no deaths among the prisoners.

The convicts' arrival in Australia coincided with the introduction of a harsher and more disciplinarian regime by the new governor. Sir Ralph Darling had taken over the governorship of New South Wales the previous year from Sir Thomas Brisbane, a man regarded as weak, inept and unable to take control of events. His lack of leadership had, in the eyes of some, started the colony on a downward spiral. The military were suffering from low morale and it was generally perceived among the ranks that the convicts had a better life. The appointment of Sir Ralph Darling was to be the remedy for an ailing administration that needed an injection of discipline. It soon became apparent that Darling was going to rule with an iron rod and within a very short time of his arrival he showed to his subordinates his intentions when he began to introduce more draconian measures.

Two of the soldiers that believed the convicts were having a better life than the military were Sudds and Thompson of the 57th Regiment. They had seen how convicts were allowed to earn enough money to make them reasonably well off and when their sentences had been completed they were able to make a fresh start and build on their new-found wealth. Sudds and Thompson decided to steal a piece of cloth from a shop in George Street, Sydney, in the knowledge they would be caught and would stand trial. They reasoned that they would be given a prison sentence, be discharged from the army and then once they had paid their dues to society they would be free of the military and in a position to take up a life of free enterprise. All went well for them; they were arrested, stood trial and were sentenced to seven years each. Unfortunately, the real motive for their robbery (namely the discontent within the military) became known and Governor Darling intervened and had the two soldiers transferred from the gaol and into military custody and the sentence was changed to seven years' hard labour in irons. As a final form of punishment, once the sentence had been completed both men were to be returned to their regiment to complete any outstanding service. The irons that they were fitted with were so small that neither man could stand up nor straighten their backs and in the case of Sudds the fittings around his arms and ankles were so tight they cut into his flesh and restricted the flow of blood. Sudds, who was already ill, died within days but remarkably Thompson survived.

For the convicts who had been transported conditions also became worse when Darling became governor. Floggings became more frequent and 'short allowances of coarse food' was reintroduced, something that had not been seen for many years. At Moreton Bay a new penal settlement was formed, with conditions so bad that the inmates would murder fellow inmates just so that they could stand trial back in Sydney and ultimately face the death penalty.

It was against this background that all the newly arrived convicts were disembarked and taken to the Hyde Park Barracks in Sydney. This was a huge, brick-built edifice that had been completed just a few years earlier using convict labour, and its three floors housed up to 1,000 convicts every single day. Complete with all the necessary utilities such as kitchens and latrines, it also came with vast dormitories for the convicts to sleep in, with every man (women were not imprisoned here until 1848) allotted a hammock each night. The guards, who at times were just as much prisoners as the convicts in this lonely outpost of the Empire, kept watch at night through holes in the dormitory walls so that order could be maintained. Should any of the criminals misbehave there was a courtroom on site to deal with them. The favoured form of punishment was flogging and this was regarded as simple and usually effective with no need to keep relatively healthy, workable convicts locked up. A two-man team would carry out each of the floggings, with a left hander being particularly prized as this allowed the 'T' to be crossed on the offender's back, making it look as if it was covered in chevron-style markings. If those carrying out the flogging felt in a vigorous mood it was quite possible to flay the skin and flesh away so that the ribs became exposed, and in many cases the resultant wound healed to leave scars that resembled a field ploughed by a madman. Any prisoner who cried out or broke down while receiving the lash was described as being 'sandstone', a title that possibly originates from the pratice of being fastened to a piece of sandstone to receive the punishment. Surrounding all this was a high, imposing wall that reinforced the belief that this was a prison within a prison.

Each of the convicts were fed and housed at Hyde Park Barracks until they could be 'assigned out', and it was in here that they would have undergone a lengthy process of documentation where all sorts of details would have been noted. Their literacy, religion, occupation, age and place of birth would all have been recorded and so would a description of their physical make-up, with notes made of their build, colour of hair and any birth marks, tattoos or scars. Those convicts with a skill were kept within the barracks and put to work on official projects, while unskilled convicts were 'assigned out' to free settlers as cheap labour for unskilled jobs. Free settlers were people who had seen the chance to make a fortune or a better life in Australia and had emigrated there voluntarily by paying their own way. Some of them were single but many were married with children and the chance of a new life in a better climate appealed to all types of people.

Whether you were assigned to a cruel or a kind master was quite literally the luck of the draw. Rules were laid down that stipulated the treatment and welfare of the convicts, including the amount food and clothing they were to be supplied with. Some of the masters treated the convicts in a very fair and humane manner, while others treated them as little more than slaves. Convicts who put in extra hours working for their masters in their own time were paid for their efforts and could use this money to buy extra food or clothing. For those fortunate enough to have a kindly employer the prospects for the future were good, with the possibility of a long and stable working environment, but for those with a cruel employer the prospects were much gloomier. It was known for some employers to pay wages at a very low rate and to force the convicts to then spend their money in the company stores buying food and provisions at an inflated rate – in effect working for nothing.

The government also set down the amount of food that each of the convicts was to receive from their masters and once again the quality and quantity depended on the attitude of the master. The regulations stipulated that each male convict should be supplied with some form of meat (usually about one pound of salt pork, beef or mutton), one or two pounds of flour or cornmeal to make damper (a type of soda bread), tea and sugar. Female convicts were issued about two thirds of this amount.

Very often the worst of the masters would only supply meat of the most inferior quality, which in most cases meant that it was far from fresh. Fruit and vegetables were not on the menu at all but for those able to get a small plot of land this was no problem. After finishing work for the day, or during their free time on Sundays, those convicts with spare time would grow their own crops to supplement their otherwise repetitive diet. In practice, the food supplied to the convicts varied widely from employer to employer and it was not at all unusual for any local produce to be used as a replacement for that stipulated in the regulations.

Officially, the convicts were to be supplied with two sets of clothing each year. The winter set consisted of a coarse woollen jacket, a waistcoat, woollen stockings, shoes, two cotton or linen shirts, a neckerchief and a woollen hat, while the summer set of clothing was almost the same as the winter set, with the slight difference being that the woollen jacket and waistcoat were replaced by a canvas shirt. The reality of the situation meant that some of the convicts were clothed in nothing better than rags, especially if their new set of clothes failed to appear, and in many cases they also went barefoot because their shoes had fallen to pieces or had worn out. Those with more benevolent masters faired much better, for they would supplement the government-issue clothing using their own money, making conditions much more comfortable for the convicts in their charge.

Bennett and Lingard were assigned out to free settlers who needed assistance to run their businesses, which were usually sheep farms, and because of the area from which they originated this should have suited them ideally. Regardless of their previous companionship and considerable time spent in confinement together, the two were not assigned to the same employer and so they were parted, never to see each other again. Future events would show what Bennett and Lingard were really like, for their lives were to take completely different paths and ultimately one of them would attain a modicum of success while the other would suffer deprivation and hardship.

For prisoners who kept out of trouble and helped in the construction of a new society the first real reward would be the offering of a 'ticket of leave'. This was official permission for husbands, wives or families to be allowed to travel out to live with the convict in a semi-free environment in which the convict was able to obtain paid work within the district. To obtain the ticket of leave the convict 'lifers' such as Lingard and Bennett had to work for three different employers over 12 years, 10 years with two employers or eight years with just one employer, and each employer had to give a good reference as to the character and steadfastness of the offender. This was then considered by the authorities and if it was thought suitable the lucky recipient would be able to enjoy a limited new-found freedom. The difficulty for any relatives that wanted to join their loved ones in Australia was that the cost of passage had to be paid for by those that were travelling. On rare occasions communities would club together to send someone out and occasionally the authorities would take pity and dip into the coffers to help – but not very often.

If, after a number of years, this same convict had continued to be a good citizen then they could be given a pardon. In the case of those given life transportation this would be a conditional pardon, which meant that they could travel anywhere in the world except back to their home country, so even with a pardon they were still in exile. An absolute pardon was rarely given to those serving a life sentence, but for those fortunate enough to be given or to earn one it gave them the ability to return to their home country – if they could afford the fare home.

Bennett's upbringing in the country must have stood him in good stead for he was assigned to a farm and in the 1828 census he is shown as being a 'servant' for William Carter, a farmer in Piercefield, New South Wales. This job title could have meant anything but more likely than not it meant that Bennett was either a shepherd or a general labourer. Piercefield was situated in the Upper Hunter Valley and was only just starting to be settled by the white immigrants and therefore only accessible by rough tracks, which at times seemed impassable. Just eight

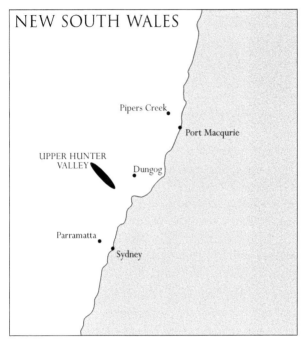

NEW SOUTH WALES

Pipers Creek•

•Port Macqurie

UPPER HUNTER
VALLEY

Dungog•

Parramatta•

•Sydney

years earlier the first of these settlers had made the move to this area and now more were joining them. Its position some distance from Sydney made it seem like a wilderness but within relative striking distance of civilisation. As the area was being 'opened up', a military post and courthouse had been built at Seaham to provide protection – and to watch the newcomers. With time, the outpost at Seaham and those like it became less on the fringes of the settled area and as the settlers ventured farther from civilisation they complained at the lack of protection and justice that the authorities could provide. One of those voicing his opinions was James Dowling, a supreme court judge who had lands in the area. He pointed out that it could be as far as 70 miles to the nearest courthouse and this gave any wayward or escaped convicts just the opportunity they longed for to evade justice. By the early 1830s local communities like Dungog had sprung up in response to this plea, bringing with them order and a sense of belonging.

William Carter was a free settler who took advantage of the chance of using cheap labour in looking after his farm and he employed many convicts in that way.[5] Bennett continued to keep on the right side of the law and by 1837 he was working for Harley Grayson of Dungog, although in what capacity is unknown. Then, on 18 February 1839 he reached a very important milestone when he was granted his ticket of leave. It had taken Bennett nearly 13 long years to achieve this and his sense of elation would have been palpable, for now in some small way he was able to choose his own destiny. He obviously had come to like the area for he made an application to the Dungog bench to be allowed to carry on living there, and just eight months later they agreed, handing him a small piece of paper with the required details filled in. It is possible that he had struck up a relationship with a local woman – if he had then that would have been another reason to stay. The granting of his ticket of leave was announced in the *Sydney Gazette* of 19 March, giving notice to all who saw it that he had reached a particular level of 'rehabilitation'. It also gave a chance for those who objected to do so.

There are no records to show whether or not any of Bennett's family travelled out to join him but the chances of that happening are extremely remote given the fact that he had probably lost all contact with them in the intervening years, and being a single man he would have had no immediate family who would feel the need to make the journey, even if they could have afforded it. His application for a ticket would have been a deserved reward for keeping out of trouble and being a useful citizen during the growth of this new nation.

The last mention of Bennett dates from 1846 (or as some records seem to indicate 1847), when he was granted a conditional pardon. This had taken over 20 years to achieve and was about the best that he could have hoped for. With the granting of his pardon, Bennett was a free man within Australia, but he was still banished from England and could only return under pain of death, something that he had escaped from once already and so would have been a fool to risk again. While he was a convict he did not ask the governor for permission to marry but it is possible he might have married after he was pardoned in 1846 as he was still a relatively young man of about 42. Sadly, at this point William Bennett passes into obscurity and his fate is unknown except that it is inconceivable that he lived and died anywhere except in his adopted home of Australia.

# THE DEFIANT ONE

Walter Lingard gives the impression of being a somewhat different character to William Bennett, for example at his trial he had tried unsuccessfully to avoid conviction by challenging the main prosecution witness, wheras Bennett put in a 'guilty' plea. When this failed Lingard appears to have accepted his fate, for his conduct was not marked by unruly behaviour. His mind would constantly have been full of thoughts about his wife, baby daughter and the life that he had left behind, something he would have longed to return to. However, the conditions on-board the hulk *Justitia* at Woolwich and the subsequent voyage on the *Speke* to Australia would have hardened his mind. It was a well-known fact that a number of convicts faced with the same conditions and prospects as Lingard became morose and depressed, with some taking their own lives, or, worse still, committing murder so that they would be executed. During his voyage on-board the *Speke* he would have received some schooling as part of the regime laid down by Alick Osborne, the surgeon in charge, and yet he remained illiterate all his life. Being relatively unskilled, his prospects for improvement in Australia seemed slim, because although weavers were needed in the new colony, their numbers were limited. By far the greatest number of workers were assigned as manual labourers to the free settlers and this was the best that Lingard could hope for.

Along with William Bennett, Lingard's arrival at Sydney would have been a cultural shock. The climate and countryside would have been completely alien to him with strange new creatures and plants all around. Once inside the barracks at Hyde Park and away from this strange new environment, his processing and registration completed, just like Bennett he would have been allocated to a settler. It was around this time that his rebellion against the prison authorities began. In the same 1828 census that shows Bennett leading the life of a servant on a farm, Lingard is shown as being on iron gang number 2, which was a form of chain gang where the convicts wore fetters and chains every single hour of the day. These heavy irons were secured in place by a blacksmith and weighed between 7lb and 9lb each. The rough edges would cut into the skin causing cuts, sores and abrasions that seldom had chance to heal. Each of the convicts was chained at the ankles and then chained to each other, with their punishment increased by halving their food ration. It was the iron gangs that built the roads and the work was hard and exhausting. Of the three types of gangs (the road parties and the bridge parties), life on the iron gang was the harshest. The men in these work parties toiled to the extreme while those in the other gangs faired a little better, with their work being less physical. The fact that Lingard was in a gang showed he had committed some serious crime during his short stay in the colony, but it seems that this was just a foretaste of what was to come.

Over the next three years Lingard settled down to a life of drudgery and his time in the gang would have been one of hard work with little rest. During these years he would have longed to be free, and in late 1831 he took his chance and escaped. The system for recapturing an escaped convict was well tried and tested, for with such an enormous convict population escapes were frequent. Once his escape had been discovered and notified to the local police office a letter would then be forwarded to the colonial secretary in Sydney giving all the details of the prisoner and listing age, physical description and any distinguishing marks (hence the reason for taking all the details of appearance at Hyde Park Barracks when the convicts first arrived in Australia). The next step would be to place an advertisement in the *Sydney Gazette* showing these details and offering a reward, usually 10s (50p), for their recapture. Twice in October his details were published for the world at large to see and within days they produced the required results and Lingard was recaptured. For escaping and having a few days of liberty he received 50 lashes, but he would not have been given any real time to get over his injuries, instead he would have been returned to work almost immediately. This form of prison environment was not seen as a place to rehabilitate wrongdoers who could be returned to society as better citizens, it was a system designed to punish and to use these unfortunates as an example in order to deter others from following the same path.

Slowly Lingard's wounds healed and eventually his time in the gangs drew to a close, yet with all his past troubles it did not stop him from overstepping the mark once again. For the next three and a half years he kept out of any serious trouble but in March 1836 he finally lost control and was caught in an affray. His punishment was swift and severe when it came and on 23 March he was sentenced to be kept in irons for 12 months. While in the gangs he had been fettered and chained, yet not too heavily to work, but his new chains would be much heavier and with restricted movement to prevent further escape. To stop a prisoner slipping out of the ankle irons, the blacksmith made their fitting permanent by riveting them in place. Every waking moment he would have to take the extra weight of iron rings around his ankles with another ring around his waist from which chains hung down to the ankle rings. In some cases convicts were 'double ironed' if it was thought that they posed a particular risk of escaping again. The belief was that the extra weight would subdue any and all thoughts that the convict might harbour towards another bid for freedom. For a full year Lingard carried the burden of the chains while carrying out his duties, which were just as demanding as before. Exactly one year to the day Lingard had his irons removed as the blacksmith beat out the rivets to remove the dead weight from his body. Perhaps his pent-up tensions spilled over or possibly one of the guards ridiculed and laughed at him, but Lingard was given 12 lashes for insolence on that very same day.

Unlike William Bennett, who did as he was told and kept his head down while slowly working his way to a form of freedom, William Lingard had taken the route of becoming a hardened criminal and all the punishments that he had endured did little to dissuade him from this course of action. Just two months after being released from the irons he was given a further 50 lashes for disorderly conduct and he topped off a turbulent year when on 27 December 1836 he received another 30 lashes for overstaying his pass. (Convicts could be given passes for short periods of freedom away from the gaol environment where they would be billeted if not assigned to an employer.)

For a while at least Lingard appears to have learnt his lesson and managed to stay out of any real trouble, and the following year he is shown as working for a John Matthews of Parramatta. In what capacity he was employed is not known, and his being assigned to Matthews would only have come following a period of relative calm or submission on his part. Parramatta, approximately 15 miles to the north-west of Sydney, had developed into a fertile farming area that helped to feed the growing population of Australia. Its open lands were reached by sailing the waters of the Parramatta river to its furthest navigable point. When the first fleet of convicts had arrived at Sydney Cove in 1788 they found that the land was unsuitable for sustaining the amount of food production that was needed to feed the soon-to-be-expanding population. The following year a convict by the name of James Ruse was given permission to farm the area on the condition that he made it a viable project, and it was Ruse who became the first person to successfully grow grain in Australia. This area was also the birthplace of the Australian woollen industry, when in the 1790s John Macarthur, who was commandant of Parramatta, set up a farm and grew wheat and farmed sheep. Later records show that Lingard's profession at one time was as a ploughman and farm labourer, and so this could have been his task at John Matthews's establishment. There is even a possibility that this is where Lingard learnt his trade because he appears to have spent most of the last nine years in chain gangs and after such a torrid time this would have been his first real opportunity to gain some self-respect from an employer who was not trying to punish him.

Employment brought with it many benefits, the simplest being a change of environment and scenery, while on the more practical side of it the willing convict would gain money and wages, be free of constraining military discipline and would generally eat better food. The downside was that they would have lower wages than a free settler and the work would and could be hard, long and at times tedious, especially to those placed in a type of work to which they were not suited or disliked. Many rules were in place to ensure that the convicts maintained discipline, even when out of the prison barracks (many of the convicts returned each night to sleep in the prison dormitories), and anyone who broke the rules would be harshly punished. Complacency or arrogance must have crept into

Lingard's behaviour for during July 1837 he ignored his curfew and stayed out of his lodgings all night. For the crime of being absent for one night he was punished by being given a total of 100 lashes. It was a punishment designed to beat him into submission and to act as a deterrent to other would-be undisciplined prisoners.

Lingard's spell of good behaviour did not last for long and within months he was once again condemned to servitude in an iron gang. His new iron gang was sent over 260 miles to the north of Sydney to the former penal colony of Port Macquarie. Originally founded in 1821 purely as a place for convicts to serve out their sentence for crimes committed in New South Wales, the colony was closed in 1830 when the region was opened up for free settlers to venture into the area. The land was marshy in parts but there were forested hills and rising slopes elsewhere. It was the good grazing land, abundance of timber and plentiful fishing that made this area prime for colonisation. For nine years the settlers had been encouraged to use this land for the production of food and it showed itself to be an increasingly popular place, with a slow but steady rise in the population in the urbanised areas. Outside of the main town of Port Macquarie the population was still sparse when Lingard arrived but given time that would change, for it was here in the 1820s that sugar cane had been grown for the first time on the whole of the continent, showing that this was a land of productivity and opportunity.

The hot, sunny, dry weather that the iron gangs endured while working on the roads would only have increased the hatred felt by most of those forced to carry out this extreme form of exertion, a relentless grind designed to crush the spirit and suppress even the most hardened of convicts. Those prisoners chained together would have plenty of time to talk of escape and imagine what it would be like to be free. Occasionally, some of these plans would explode into action and the convicts would make a dash into the wild countryside in the hope of escape. As they were chained together, these small groups of men would take the first opportunity they could to rid themselves of their heavy irons and fetters and either merge into the background or become bushrangers – wild, unruly escapees, some of whom committed some of the worst atrocities imaginable in their bid to stay free.

On 29 June 1839 during one of their days toiling near Port Macquarie, and less than two weeks after joining the gang, Lingard and his fellow convicts took their chance, broke away from their captors and, making their way into the untamed countryside that surrounded them, quickly melted away. They were now in a completely unknown environment, with no food or water to sustain them. With Lingard were five others, each one with their own reason for escape. The youngest of the escapees was Samuel Faith at just 25 years old, while the oldest was Robert Taylor at 36. Neither Faith's profession as a seaman nor Taylor's as a merchant's clerk would give them any advantage in the outback and they would be reliant on working together to stay free. The other three of Lingard's companions were James Brian (a shoemaker), Michael Darcy (a labourer) and John Williamson, who was probably the ringleader, for he was a former soldier who been sent to Australia five years earlier to serve a life sentence after committing mutiny while stationed in Ireland. This tall, young Scotsman had shown his true character years before while still in the army when he was sentenced to four months imprisonment and 250 lashes for breaking army regulations. All of the prisoners had suffered injuries before their escape, with Lingard having a crippled little finger on his left hand after having an accident with a reaping hook, which further re-enforces the evidence that his employment at Parramatta the previous year had been on a farm. The rest of his companions carried a whole variety of scars and burn marks to show just how tough their existence was.

During their flight into the wilderness they may have overpowered their guards because it is reported that they soon had firearms, and only two days later they made their way to Pipers Creek, a little river with isolated settlers' farmsteads dotted around. There they entered the house of a Mr Allen and proceeded to ransack it while turning on Allen and beating him mercilessly, breaking his arm and several other bones. Their lust for cruelty and profit not satiated, they left Allen to his fate and made their way to the property of a Mr Steele, which again they plundered and ransacked. Finding that the owner of the property was absent, they turned on the overseer, physically abusing him and forcing him to show them the road that led to the harbour on the Maria River. Should they be able to steal a boat it would hasten their escape, for the Maria flowed into the Hastings River and then to the sea past Port Macquarie, a route that could have given them access to the whole of the Australian east coast should they risk using it. Alternatively, they could choose to sail further up the Maria and into the unknown regions of the outback.

Following the directions given to them by the overseer, they made their way to the harbour where they took the local constable prisoner, using his own handcuffs to restrain him. Taking the constable with them, they all set off to find a boat; however, their plans began to fall apart when the constable managed to break free of them and escaped. The convicts fired a number of shots after him, but being fit and active the constable was able to avoid injury and hurriedly put distance between himself and the fugitives.

As reports began to filter back about the whereabouts of the convicts, the police in Port Macquarie started to organise search parties. The chief constable himself set off in pursuit at the head of three strong parties of special constables to join the military parties that were also searching for Lingard and his companions. The district of Port Macquarie only had three paid constables at that time and none of these were mounted so most of the 'specials' would have been a number of the more trustworthy convicts. It was an accepted practice for convicts to be allowed this responsibility, for not all of the prisoners who were transported were hardened criminals. Many of them were ordinary people who had fallen foul to an overly harsh legal system, and these were the type of men that the police turned to at times like this.

Such was the violence being shown by the escaped convicts that the police regarded them as being '…of the worst character sent to this district to work on the roads.' This led the local police magistrate to take the unprecedented step of issuing a reward of 10 pounds for the capture of each of the four worst characters, namely William Lingard, John Williamson, Michael Darcy and James Brian. The usual reward for information leading to the capture of escaped prisoners was still 10 shillings (50p) each, and although the size of the reward had not increased in many years, it was still seen as a large sum of money. The reward of 10 pounds for the return of each of the worst convicts was an astronomically high sum and was designed to induce assistance from all quarters. Should another convict capture those who had escaped the police magistrate promised to strongly recommend them for a conditional pardon, a promise designed to appeal to even the most hardened of criminals.

By 4 July the search was in full swing and a letter was on its way from the police magistrate at Port Macquarie to the colonial secretary in Sydney, giving all the details of the events so far and asking for the proposed reward to be sanctioned and funded, as well as backing the local police magistrate in his offer of a conditional pardon. The colonial secretary agreed to all of the proposals in the letter and instructed his office to insert an advertisement in the *Sydney Gazette* giving all the known details about the convicts. It took until 7 August for all the information to be gathered and by then the convicts had been on the loose for over a month. All this time the police and the military had doggedly kept up the chase for the escaped men, who were still together as one group.

Before the advertisement could be placed in the newspaper, events took an unexpected turn when Lingard and his comrades were tracked down and cornered. Instead of surrendering meekly, however, the convicts decided to make a fight of it. During the ensuing gunfight one of their number was shot through the shoulder, thereby bringing resistance to an end. The others, seeing their fallen comrade, decided that discretion was the better part of valour and all of them immediately surrendered, ready to face the consequences. All six convicts, including the wounded man, were taken into custody and securely locked away in gaol to await their fate. True to his word, the police magistrate offered a conditional pardon to two of the special constables who were convicts themselves. Constable George Smith was granted his pardon on 1 November; however, Constable Murphy declined his pardon on the grounds that he was due to be set free the following month and he would prefer to have his portion of the £40 reward which was to be shared among the military – his wish was granted.

The six captured men spent the next few weeks in the all-too-familiar surroundings of the gaol waiting for their trial to begin amid tight security, and they would probably have been wearing the hated chains. With their past history it is probable that they were double chained to stop them from trying to escape again. Their appearance at the Supreme Court in Sydney was, in effect, only a formality. With no real defence available to them, it came as no real surprise when on 11 November Lingard was sentenced to 15 years' transportation to Norfolk Island. His main conviction was for 'house robbery' and the taking of money, plate and wearing apparel, the other crimes possibly appeared less important and harder to prove. Of the six men who had escaped and had later been recaptured only one was to stay in Sydney, and that was John Williamson the ex-soldier. Being a former soldier and used to firearms, he was most probably the convict at the forefront in the shoot-out and was possibly the one that had been shot in the shoulder. By the time of the trial his wounds would not have healed and with the severity of such an injury there was a distinct possibility he might not have survived.

Within weeks, Lingard and the others would be on their way to Norfolk Island, which at that time was described as a 'hell in paradise'.

# HELL IN PARADISE

Thirteen years had passed since William Lingard had first arrived in Australia and his former existence back in Litton must have been a distant memory, with his wife and child appearing to come from another life. During his time as a convict he had missed many family events, both happy and sad. In 1827, the year after he was transported, his younger brother Samuel had married Mary Barson and just 12 months later Mary had given birth to Hannah, their daughter receiving the same name as William's own little girl. Despite this happy event, the name of Lingard was not well respected and their

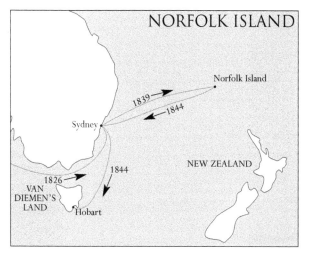

notorious reputation was added to when in that same year his older sister, another Hannah, gave birth to her second illegitimate child, George.

In 1830 the family suffered tragedy when Samuel's wife Mary died shortly after giving birth to Dinah, but within the week Dinah had also died, leaving Samuel to bring up his surviving daughter alone. The sympathy that this tragedy brought out would not have lasted too long, however, for within months the Lingard reputation had once again taken a turn for the worse when Hannah yet again brought an illegitimate child into the world. Her new baby son, James, would grow up to be yet another Lingard who brought shame to the family name. The family's year of misfortune and shame was compounded when William's younger sister Elizabeth also gave birth to an illegitimate daughter, Eliza.

All these events had been witnessed by Anthony Lingard the elder and his wife Elizabeth, and as they looked at the events that had overtaken their family they must have wondered what it was that had brought them to this point: one son executed for murder, another transported to a far-off land, never to return, four of their own children dying in infancy and no less than four illegitimate grandchildren.

Socially and economically the country was finding that things were slowly improving. The continued industrialisation of the cities and towns was destroying the health of those that lived in them and the generally increased affluence of the population was centred on the upper and middle classes who resided there and in their country houses. The truly destitute had no real chance of escaping the economic trap but for the rest there was always hope. In the countryside unemployment was high, even the migration away from the land and into the factories had not been able to stem this trend, with events coming to head in 1830 with the 'Swing Riots'. The riots were led by the mysterious and elusive Captain Swing and spread across the south of England, East Anglia and the Midlands, and they have since been described as 'the last Labourers' Revolt'. There was very little violence, though, and the riots mainly consisted of the burning of hayricks and the destruction of threshing machines. The main aim of the rioters was to demand action on the high price of bread and to bring about an increase in wages and higher rates of relief for the poor. Brutal measures were used to put down the riots, with nine men being hanged, 457 transported and a great number more imprisoned.

While the judicial system was still unsympathetic and at times vindictive, it was generally becoming more inclined to toleration and understanding. The sentences handed out for minor offences were still harsh but they were less harsh than they had been for many years.

Both Anthony and Elizabeth were getting old and the mental and physical strain of bringing up a large and extended family would have taken its toll, and it came as no real surprise when in 1835 Elizabeth died leaving Anthony to continue as sole head of the household. Anthony carried on alone for another three years until he also died, completely oblivious to William Lingard's conduct as a convict and thankfully with no possible idea of what was in store for his son.

Unaware of any of the events back in his home village, William Lingard was marched out of the gaol in Sydney and, along with his fellow prisoners from the iron gang, he was put on-board a convict ship bound for Norfolk Island. This ship was full of convicts who had reoffended while in New South Wales and now they were being sent to the one place that they all feared.

Norfolk Island had first been occupied by Europeans when the British set up a colony there in 1788, with the population eventually being made up of convicts and military guards, with some of the convicts who had served their time staying on as free settlers. It was thought that the land was fertile enough to make the island self-sufficient in food and that the wooded lands would provide timber for ships' masts. Unfortunately, however, an experiment to grow flax failed, the timber proved inferior for its needs and most food crops that were produced were ravaged by rats and caterpillars. For years the government ignored advice that the colony was impractical to run, even though the evidence for closure was overwhelming. It had no natural protected harbour for shipping and communication with the mainland was difficult as Sydney was over 750 miles away. With a population that at times numbered over 1,000, it was finally decided to evacuate everyone and to close the colony. In 1814 the last of the prisoners left the island after making sure all the remaining buildings had been destroyed so that other colonial powers could not use them and thus set up their own outpost. Norfolk Island remained abandoned and desolate until 1825, when it was decided to rebuild the island as a penal colony for the worst offenders.

It was determined that Norfolk Island should be the ultimate place of punishment, with virtually no chance of ever leaving, and that the punishments which were to be inflicted upon the inmates were only to be one step short of death. This regime was supposed to act as a deterrent to any other would-be offenders and was not designed to reform the character of those incarcerated there. As each governor took over from his predecessor the treatment of the prisoners deteriorated by degrees, with prisoners being worked in irons and floggings part of normality. In 1834 there had been a riot on the island and when it was finally subdued a number of the convicts who had taken part were sentenced to death. In order to provide comfort and solace to the condemned, Father William Ullathorne, the Vicar General of Sydney, made the long sea voyage to the penal colony and found that he had the odious task of telling those condemned who would be reprieved and who would die. He was shocked to find that those who received a reprieve broke down and cried uncontrollably, while those that were to die thanked God. These were the conditions that Lingard and his fellow escapees were heading to.

Shortly after Lingard's arrival on Norfolk Island he had perhaps his first real piece of good fortune when a new governor was appointed. Alexander Maconochie was a man with a belief that convicts should be reformed and not punished. His plan was to reward good behaviour and not to continually impose harsher punishments in the hope of providing a deterrent. His authority to try out his new reforms was limited to the 'new hands', prisoners new to the island, while the 'old hands' were to be kept under the existing system – and both groups were to be kept separated. Maconochie soon ignored his orders and used his new reward-based system on all the convicts, and this could be one of the reasons why Lingard began to be less troublesome. Living conditions on the island remained appalling and just months after arriving one of Lingard's fellow escapees from the iron gang, James Brian, died of dysentery.

For over four years Lingard survived without creating trouble. His criminal record for the time he spent at Norfolk Island says quite simply 'nil', possibly a testament to Maconochie's reform ideas coupled with strict and watchful guards. Discipline among the prisoners was still at the forefront of penal colony life and even with the reforms in place it took a strong character to survive. By 1846, once Maconochie had left his post as governor, it was noted that flogging and torture were commonplace, food was scarce and of poor quality, the housing was totally inadequate, convicts were insubordinate and the overseers corrupt. It was Lingard's sheer good fortune to be one of those lucky enough to avoid the decline into an almost lawless prison environment when he and many of the convicts were moved to another penal colony before the slip towards anarchy began.

In 1844 it was decided that many of the convicts should be moved from Norfolk Island to Van Diemen's Land after it had been decided to transfer jurisdiction of the island from New South Wales to that of the government of Van Diemen's Land. Norfolk Island did not cease to be a penal colony until 1855 so Lingard was indeed fortunate to be able to rid himself of this tortuous little island so quickly.

On 18 May 1844 William Lingard, Samuel Faith and 148 more of his fellow convicts were embarked on the government barque *Lady Franklin*. This specially made, sturdy little three-masted wooden ship of just 270 tons had been entirely made using convict labour at the government ship yard at Port Arthur in Van Diemen's Land less than three years before. At just 90ft in length from stem to stern and having only two decks, space on-board was at a premium. With the convicts being herded onto the gently rolling deck under the watchful eye of the ship's master, Captain Willett, the military guards would have to be prepared for any unrest. The army's presence on this voyage was a strong one, with 24 rank and file members of the 51st and 96th Regiments under the nominal command of Ensign Singleton there to keep order, not only during the period of embarkation but also throughout the voyage. The ship's crew, which usually numbered in the region of nine, including the master, watched as one by one the convicts took their places below decks, readying themselves for the voyage ahead. For all of those on the ship the conditions were uncomfortable as the *Lady Franklin* made its way across the open ocean. With the rolling and pitching of the ship and the cramped surroundings endured by all those on-board, sickness and disease was something that was feared by anyone unfortunate enough to be in this situation and was why the government had sent one more special passenger on the trip. To avoid the possibility of an outbreak of illness and to ensure the welfare of the convicts, Dr James Agnew had been employed to travel on all the convict ships that transported prisoners from Norfolk Island to Van Diemen's Land. James Agnew was a competent physician who applied himself diligently to his job, and when his time as a government official came to an end he turned his mind to many years of political service. The doctor's presence brought the total number of those on-board this small vessel to approximately 185.

Unbeknown to those on-board, the *Lady Franklin* appeared to bear a charmed life and had endured a catalogue of mishaps and unfortunate events in the recent past that almost equalled those endured by William Lingard during his time as a convict. In August 1842, less than a year after being launched, the *Lady Franklin* was heading south from Waterloo Point on the east coast of Van Diemen's Land when it struck some uncharted rocks off the Hippolytes, an area close to the Tasman Peninsular on the south-east corner of the island. As water poured in through the damaged hull, the passengers and crew furiously worked at the pumps to keep the water from rising too high and sinking the ship. The captain managed to steer the stricken vessel into the Port Arthur penal settlement and safely run it aground close to the ship builders where it had originally been built. All 93 passengers and crew were able to breathe a collective sigh of relief at their lucky escape.

Captain Willet himself also became a victim of the *Lady Franklin*'s chain of mishaps when he was suspended for displaying the Saint George's ensign at the masthead. A regular naval officer had noticed this breach of regulations and had made a formal complaint. The resultant enquiry established that the flag had been run up the mast by one of the mates to air and that the captain was innocent of any wrongdoing. There is no record as to the fate of the ship's mate.

Perhaps the most significant event to happen to this little ship occurred a few days before Christmas 1853 when on a voyage from Hobart to Norfolk Island carrying convicts and, strangely enough, a consignment of postage stamps. After some days out at sea, the convicts mutinied, took over the ship and escaped taking with them the postage stamps as a prize. There is no record of the convicts being successfully recaptured but ironically enough a number of the stamps did turn up some time later.

The *Lady Franklin* carried out its duties as a convict transport until 1855, when it was sold off to become a whaling ship and renamed the *Emily Downing*. Between 1858 (after its refitting and conversion) and 1883 the *Emily Downing* completed 25 whaling voyages before being turned into a hulk in 1885 when it became a floating store for explosives. It was during one of its whaling expeditions in 1864 that tragedy struck when the ship's master, Captain Lucas, and five other crew members were washed overboard, never to be seen again.

There are two versions of the story of the ship's final demise: in one account this little ship carried out its duties as a hulk until 1907 when it was broken up, while in a contradictory report the ship was beached and wrecked in 1900. Regardless of the real ending, this small wooden vessel performed its duties for many decades and outlived all those that boarded the ship with Lingard and Faith.

Lingard's other partners in crime from the iron gang had to wait some time for their turn to leave Norfolk Island. Michael Darcy embarked in November the following year, while Robert Taylor, the last of the surviving quartet, left in August 1846 after enduring some of the worst conditions to prevail on the island.

The *Lady Franklin*'s route to Van Diemen's Land first saw the convicts making the week-long voyage back to Sydney and then taking the final leg to their new home, finally landing at Hobart on 6 June. When convicts were transferred between gaols it was the duty of the prisoner to inform the authorities of the new penal establishment of their original crime so that new records could be made. William Lingard's ego must have grown during his period of transportation (or possibly his embarrassment due to the nature of his original conviction) because he reported to the surgeon of the *Lady Franklin* a slightly exaggerated crime to the one he actually committed. In his report in the log the surgeon noted that Lingard was sentenced at Derby to life transportation for highway robbery on a Mr Baggs and that he relieved Baggs of 50 pounds. In reality, Lingard and Bennett had netted a total of £2 1s 0d (£2.05p) and one pocket book between them. The crimes he committed while on the run from the iron gang he reported correctly – perhaps these filled the necessary criteria to enhance his standing. The surgeon also noted the names of Lingard's parents and some of his siblings; perhaps Lingard thought they were all still alive at that time. Most poignantly, there is one entry under the column headed 'Married or Single' that simply says 'M. 1 child'. For all his failings, this long-term criminal still remembered the wife and daughter he had left behind all those years ago.

The arrival of the *Lady Franklin* at Hobart should have ushered in a new era in Lingard's life. As elsewhere in Australia the conditions that the convicts lived and worked in were at times appalling, but here in Van Diemen's Land there was at least the chance of a slightly better situation. Situated off the south coast of Australia, this large island had infinitely more space than Norfolk Island, and Hobart on its south-east corner offered a gateway to the interior where work was available to those willing to put their minds to the task. Free settlers had been encouraged to populate the island and farms were springing up all over the region. The so-called 'Black War' of earlier years had faded away and the land was now more peaceful. When European settlers had first come to the island a conflict had erupted in which the Europeans and indigenous local populations had fought in a head-to-head conflict to see who could gain control of the land. In the 1820s the wars were at their most intense and by the 1830s they were all but over, leaving the land free for the settlers to use as their own. This freedom of movement meant that farming and other industries had a chance to get a foothold, which was seen as a good way to provide employment to the convicts. In Hobart and Port Arthur various factories and work establishments, including ship building, were set up to give work to the prisoners. Those with skills were highly prized and employers would very often overlook minor transgressions such as drunkenness so that magistrates would not assign the convict elsewhere. Food rations were regarded as generous and a large number of convicts married and had families. In general there were no bars on the windows and many of the convicts lived in cottages and not prison cells. For those that were unskilled in any particular profession the prospects were not all bad either. Work on the roads or another capitol project was to be their employment, and although it was far from easy work, it was at least less intense and cruel than in most other places. At times punishment could (and would) be hard and swift so obeying the rules was a sensible decision, for when infringements took place the sentences handed down could be extreme.

The more benign penal regime that Alexander Maconochie had partially introduced at Norfolk Island might have helped Lingard but his arrival on Van Diemen's Land seems to have once again turned him against the system. Perhaps his new-found greater freedom had given him a sense of arrogance, for within weeks of arriving in his new home he was once again in trouble.

By late September 1844 he was once more serving six months' hard labour at Wedge Bay, south-east of Hobart, for insolence, with the first month to be served in solitary confinement. In Van Diemen's Land, to be placed in the iron gang was not a common punishment so Lingard's behaviour must have been extreme. While in the gang he continued to be a source of trouble and he was not finally released from it until October the following year.

On 7 December 1845 he was assigned to the prison barracks in Hobart, a huge series of brick-built buildings that had within its complex a church, church hall, cells and dormitories for both male and female convicts, workshops (including a flour mill), kitchens, courtrooms and a myriad of other buildings to help run the gaol efficiently. In the distance overlooking the gaol were the tall hills that dominated the whole of the area giving it a sense of isolation and seclusion, while on the seaward side of town the waters of the bay meandered around large islands as they made their way to the open sea.

Lingard's allocation to the barracks was primarily because he had no outside employment, but all that changed two days later when he received the first of three assignments which were to keep him usefully and almost peaceably occupied throughout the following year.

The convicts on Van Diemen's Land were all graded in a form of class system whereby those with the best record of behaviour were regarded as class-one workers, while those with the worst records were class six. Convicts in the highest class could expect better conditions, wages and possibly more freedom than those in the lower classes, with each successive drop in class receiving fewer privileges until those in class six gained only a fraction of those higher up the scale. Lingard's arrival on the island saw him enjoying the highest possible amount of privileges allowed by a convict, for his previous behaviour on Norfolk Island had earned him a class-one status. Even after his conviction for insubordination shortly after arriving on Van Diemen's Land, he had retained his class-one status as this was based partly on his approach to work. Unfortunately, within months of his release from the gang Lingard's good conduct began to lapse and it was on 15 February 1846 that he was dropped into the second class of convicts. This drop by no means implies that Lingard was violent or disruptive, instead it is more than probable that he found his new employment or employer less than fulfilling and his frustration might have shown itself in his work. For a further three months his demeanour deteriorated slightly until in May he was reduced to third class, and here he stayed with no further slumps in his ranking.

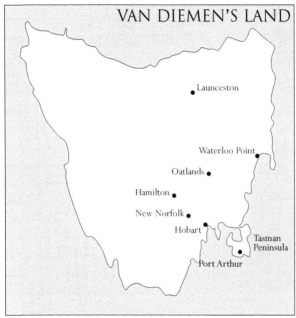

During September 1846 Lingard was given his third assignment and took up his new employment on 18 September. He knew that if he could impress his new master he would be eligible for his ticket of leave, something that would give him a whole new outlook on life, for at last he would be on his way to freedom. As he went about his daily tasks he was completely oblivious to the events taking place in his former home of Litton.

The family name of Lingard was still stained with the reputation gained by the murderer Anthony, the highwayman

William and the conduct of some of their other siblings. It was to suffer a further blow when James Lingard, the youngest illegitimate son of Hannah, was accused of making a deliberate and violent attack on a young girl.

Just two days after William had started at his new employment on the other side of the world, Mary Ann Walker was making her way to Sunday school at Litton with her brother. As the pair travelled the footpath across a field, James Lingard, who was some distance away, called out, frightening Mary so much that she began to run. Leaving her brother behind, Mary tried to put some distance between Lingard and herself but Lingard soon caught up and threw her to the ground. As Lingard attacked her '…with intent then and there violently and against her will feloniously to ravish and carnally know' she struggled and fought back, screaming and shouting for help. Nearby, Robert Walker (who was no relation) heard the screams and, shouting out, he went to investigate the commotion. While crossing the field on his way to where the noise appeared to come from, he saw Lingard and Mary getting up from behind a wall and in an instant Lingard was off and running.

Soon, Walker was with Mary and as she stood in her dirty and dishevelled clothing she told her rescuer how Lingard had tried to molest her. It was obvious that the girl was deeply distressed and Walker took her to her uncle, Francis Bromley, in the hope that he could help. When they arrived at Bromley's, Mary once again told her story, with it becoming plain to see that the girl was telling the truth and that she had not been a willing participant. The local authorities were called for and immediately searched out James Lingard to arrest him. Once found, they took him into custody and with all due haste he was taken to Derby gaol to await trial. At the October assizes, Mr Nesfield, the prosecutor, called his witnesses one by one and soon the case against Lingard built up. With no defence counsel, Lingard's chances for acquittal were virtually non-existent and the only defence he could muster was his own testimony. In it he recalled how he and Mary had been some way from any road and that she was playing truant from school '…for the purpose of getting nuts'. There was no real attempt to mount any defence, nor any probability of one being available to this untrained, naive youth, who had to conduct his own proceedings. With the judicial system stacked up against him, this young man was completely out of his depth.

The outcome was a foregone conclusion and with the jury returning a guilty verdict he was sentenced to three months of hard labour. James Lingard was only 15 years old and his victim about 10. If this case had happened 20 years earlier he would have been transported to Australia, just as his uncle William had been. However, he could have been facing the hangman had he committed this crime 40 years before, just as his uncle Anthony had done. James Lingard was a very fortunate boy indeed.

While James was paying his debt to society William was steadily increasing his chances of obtaining his ticket of leave by working hard and refraining from getting into any serious trouble. Eventually, fortune smiled on him and in April 1847 he was granted his prize and was given his much sought-after ticket. It had taken over 21 years for him to take the first step to freedom and now the extra privileges that his ticket brought would be like a breath of fresh air.

For two more years Lingard steadily worked and enjoyed his new-found sense of respectability, yet below the surface there still lurked a man who resented authority and would risk everything to hit back. In July 1849 he made the mistake of trying to help a friend escape punishment by breaking the law himself. He offered a bribe to someone to give evidence at the trial of his friend in which he was in no way connected. The police heard about Lingard's involvement and duly took him into custody. At his hearing he was sentenced to hard labour but the bitterest blow came when it was recommended that his ticket of leave be cancelled. Within four days of his conviction he was again incarcerated at the prison barracks, and for the next nine months he alternated his time between here and the Old Wharf, an area of the town that overlooked the hustle and bustle of the docks, with the large sailing ships coming and going as the winds and tides dictated. Soldiers, convicts and free settlers worked and mingled together on the dockside as they each went about their duties with the clutter of working life strewn about them, the noise and clatter of the ships loading and unloading and the constant smell of the sea filling their nostrils.

Both penal establishments were run on strict guidelines and regardless of a prisoner's status they were expected to adhere to the rules implicitly. Even those convicts who were using the gaols as sleeping accommodation and not as a place of punishment had to comply with all the prevailing rules. Lingard was indeed fortunate that his ticket was not cancelled in the end and after his sentence was served he was sent to work for a new master. Yet again his volatile character came to the fore when after only four days he was again in court for misconduct. This time he refused to hire himself out to his new employer for £10 per year and stated that '…if he liked he could please himself as to whether he worked or not'. Once more he was found guilty and once more he was sentenced to hard labour, this time for three months. It was on 26 February 1850, a mere nine days after his latest conviction, that his ticket of leave was formally revoked. Unpleasant as it was, Lingard was used to the privations of hard labour but the loss of his ticket must have been a very bitter pill to swallow.

The hardships that Lingard and his fellow convicts endured have gone down in the annals of criminal history as some of the worst to be continually administered in a modern society, yet it did nothing to break the spirit of some of the convicts, Lingard among them. The vast majority of the convicts accepted their fate and, not wanting to cause more trouble for themselves, followed the system. Some tried to beat the system and were eventually beaten and punished into submission, while a few escaped, never to be seen again. There was one group of men who did not fit into any of these categories and Lingard was one of these. These were men who refused to bow to the system and yet stayed with it to the very end.

William Lingard had undergone more punishments and hardships than most men could endure in a lifetime, but if he had only stayed out of trouble for just a few more days his ticket of leave would still have been in place and the next step would have been to receive a conditional pardon – in effect, he would have been a free man. He never knew that in October 1848 he had been recommended for a conditional pardon, which had been refused simply because of his conviction for attempted bribery of a witness. The wheels of government grind very slowly on occasions and it was the lethargy on the part of the administrators in processing the application for a pardon that allowed Lingard the time to take up his criminal activities again. Had the pardon been approved earlier, Lingard would have been effectively free and away from the many unlawful influences that surrounded him.

With his ticket of leave revoked, Lingard once more appeared to sink into his old ways, when in November 1850 he was again in court. Lingard was assigned to a Mr Warrior of Hamilton, a farming area nearly 50 miles north-west of Hobart, which was well serviced and had the land divided, with the settlement being well established and having its own church and a small but bustling community. While at Warrior's establishment, Lingard was accused of stealing some soap and with his past record he was committed for trial. Two days after his committal he was once more behind bars and for nearly the whole of the next two months he underwent the same rigorous regime of penal servitude that had dominated his life before. The gaol at New Norfolk was situated in the Derwent Valley, a picturesque part of the country halfway between Hamilton and Hobart, and here Lingard waited for his trial.

The day of the trial slowly approached and on 13 January 1851 Lingard stood in the dock. The evidence was presented to the court and for the first time in his entire life William Lingard was found not guilty of committing a crime. With the case against him discharged, Lingard was once more able to take up useful employment; however, for the moment he had to return to the prison barracks until a suitable employer could be found. New assignments soon followed, giving him the confidence he needed to regain a position of worth and to contemplate re-applying for a ticket of leave.

In June he made a formal request for a ticket and was greatly disappointed when his application was turned down. The blow was softened when he was advised that he should make another submission in six months' time. During the following months Lingard carried out his duties as instructed and to his great delight on 16 December 1851 he was once again granted his ticket of leave. For the second time in nearly five years he had achieved his goal and now he could look forward to the possibility of gaining a conditional pardon, something that would take patience and fortitude to gain. With such a prize in his sights, Lingard should have learnt his lesson and taken the prudent course of action of being cautious and reserved, but, true to his personality, he relapsed and was yet again charged with misconduct. It had taken him only three months to seriously step out of line and he must have feared for his treasured ticket of leave, and the thought of its loss must have played heavily on his mind.

Thankfully, Lingard was not reprimanded and he was able to continue his work at Oatlands, a town in the centre of Van Diemen's Land, which was originally set up as a military base for the control of convicts who were sent to work on settlements and on building roads, bridges and public buildings in the area. William Lingard's charge of misconduct was quickly forgotten when, on 22 June 1852, after nearly 26 years in Australia, he was granted his conditional pardon. How or why Lingard was allowed his pardon so quickly after gaining his ticket of leave will never be known. Perhaps someone saw a spark of goodness that deserved to be rewarded and took a chance on him, or possibly he had just served his time and now it was his turn to be free. Whatever the reason for his pardon, Lingard was now free to do just as he wished and go anywhere he wished, except back to England – to do so would mean the death penalty.

# AFTERWARDS

William Bennett, Hannah Bocking and the two Lingard brothers had committed crimes and had paid the price for their actions, whether the penalty imposed is the correct one or not is a matter of personal opinion. Their ultimate fate as criminals is well documented, but what about all the people who were affected by their actions? The victims' families and their own families who were left behind had to carry on somehow, they had to continue with their own lives and do their best to put the past behind them if they could. Those who witnessed the events as they unfolded and played their part in the judicial system also had a future to look forward to, but what actually happened to those caught up in the aftermath?

The family most affected was that of Anthony Lingard the elder, as we have seen. With the stigma of having a murderer and a highway robber in the family it would have been prudent for them to keep a low profile, yet they did exactly the opposite. With a number of illegitimate children and an accusation of an attempted sexual assault to stain the family name, it would seem reasonable to assume that the Lingard family were regarded with a certain amount of disrespect and possibly ridicule. The local parish registers show that the entries for the Lingard family gradually fell over the subsequent years, which leads to the conclusion that the remaining family members gradually moved away. There is a possibility that some of the succeeding generation moved to Sheffield, as one branch of the family seems to have come from that area. The name of Lingard also appears in greater numbers in records from the Chesterfield area, and perhaps industrialisation forced many of the family off the land and into the factories. Certainly, some of the women married and changed their names but gradually the family name faded from the local records. James Lingard, who as a young man served three months of hard labour after assaulting Mary Ann Walker, grew up to marry and have a family of his own, hopefully putting his past experiences behind him.

But who was the mysterious young woman that was carrying Anthony Lingard the younger's child and gave the vital evidence against him in court? There were eight illegitimate children baptised in Tideswell during 1815, one of which can be discounted immediately because the baptism took place on New Year's Day, which is too early in the year to be the child in question. Of the rest, one was the wife of a soldier from Belper who gave birth in the area, so it seems reasonable to discount this woman, which leaves four women from Tideswell itself, one from Grindlow (another local village) and the most obvious candidate, Grace Wager from Litton.

Grace had her fatherless daughter baptised on 30 May, giving her the name Mary Hannah. Was she called Hannah in memory of Hannah Oliver, the victim of Lingard? At the gibbeting of Lingard's body one of the constables sworn in was

Sampson Wager, which poses the question: was Sampson related to Grace? Wager is not a common surname and he could have been doing something that he felt correct in the circumstances. Sampson Wager had performed the duties of constable before so he would have known what was required of him. With Grace and Lingard coming from the same village all the probabilities show that Grace Wager was the one who gave Lingard up to the authorities.

The contrast between the struggling lower classes and the well-to-do was nowhere more apparent than at Lingard's trial. After spending his time in the gaol he was taken to the Shire Hall and stood before a judge who would have a far different future ahead of him. The judge, the Honourable Sir John Bayley, was to have a distinguished career presiding over many trials and even becoming an author when he penned the wonderfully titled book *On the Law of Bills of Exchange*. Today, it might be seen as amusing to be remembered for such a book but back then it enhanced his standing and he was later honoured to be made a Baron of the Exchequer. In 1834 he was created the 1st Baronet Bayley when he retired from the bench and shortly afterwards he was honoured by being made a privy counsellor. Bayley lived on until 1841 when he passed away at his home in Vine House near Sevenoaks, Kent, at the ripe old age of 78.

But what became of the judges who presided over the cases of Hannah Bocking and William Lingard and were willing to pass on the harsh penalties that the law proscribed?

Sir James Burrough, who presided over the trial of Hannah Bocking, had been in the law profession all his working life and yet did not take his place on the bench until 1816, by which time he was 66 years of age. Throughout his career he had the reputation of being patient and strictly impartial, and he gained a particular renown for his kindness and the simple manner in which he conducted himself, taking time to explain points of law to the jury. Burrough continued to act as a judge until he retired through ill health at the age of 79 after suffering a number of seizures while in court. He finally passed away 10 years later in 1839.

The last of the trio of judges, Sir Joseph Littledale, who oversaw the case against William Lingard and William Bennett, was born in 1767 to wealthy parents and it was after completing his education at St John's College, Cambridge, that he entered into his chosen job within the legal profession. In 1824 he was appointed to the King's Bench and worked with, among others, Sir John Bayley. His time on the bench earned him many plaudits from his colleagues, not only for his legal knowledge but also for the way in which his manner was always one of patience and kindness. At the age of 74 he retired to take up the same position that his friend Sir John Bayley had enjoyed, that of privy counsellor, but within 18 months he had succumbed to frailty and died at his home on 26 June 1842.

All of the judges died within three years of each other and all were described as being knowledgeable, honest and fair, yet there is a distinct contrast between their upbringing and that of the people they tried in court. Those that they had seen in court had a poor upbringing and were doomed to end their lives prematurely at the end of a rope or in a far-off country after suffering countless hardships with no hope of return, while each of the judges had a long life and passed away in the comfort of their own homes. The social system of the day appears to be biased towards the wealthy and well educated, with those of lower standing caught in the vicious circle of poverty that the upper classes could not understand.

William Newton, who had been at the gibbeting and had witnessed Anthony Lingard the elder watching his son's body put on public display, continued to live in the area before dying in 1830 at the age of 80. He was outlived by his beloved wife Helen, to whom he had been married for 52 years, by just eight days. William Newton rests in the cemetery of Tideswell's parish church, the same cemetery that Jane Grant, the victim of Hannah Bocking, also rests in. Sadly, he died before his wish to see gibbeting abolished came about, which thanks to his efforts and of those like him was finally realised in 1834, two years after the final event of its kind had taken place. Public opinion had finally swayed the government to take action following the practice's fall from favour.

The last two cases of gibbeting in England both took place in 1832 but even by this time the spectacle was becoming a rare event. In County Durham, William Jobling was executed and his body duly put on display as directed, but the general public's frenzy to see his exhibited body was sickening. Tourists flocked from miles around to get a view of Jobling's body and the demand was such that the local boat owners set up sightseeing trips for the purpose. After six weeks of watching this appalling behaviour, Jobling's family secretly took his body down for burial. It was in Leicester that the very last case of gibbeting took place: the murderer James Cook's body was raised up on a 33ft-high pole at the junction of Saffron Lane and Aylestone Road and the crowds immediately gathered. Such was the crush of people wanting to view the body, coupled with the revulsion felt by the locals living in the area to having this display on their doorstep, that within three days the Home Office issued instructions that Cook's body should be removed. Far from acting as a deterrent, the last two case of gibbeting had provided a means of entertainment and had become tourist attractions.

But what of Jane Grant the elder who had lost two grown-up daughters, one to natural causes and one to a scheming murderess? She lived on in her home in Litton until she passed away in late 1822. The parish records show that she was buried on 1 December at the grand old age of 73, a more than likely exaggerated figure given the age of her children. Bearing in mind that neither her relatives nor her neighbours would really know her true age it would appear to have been a well-meaning guess. Birth certificates were not introduced until 1837 and up to that point any documentation relating to births, deaths and marriages relied on someone's memory to supply the relevant details.

Of those associated with William Lingard, perhaps the most successful and accomplished was the superintendent surgeon on the convict ship *Speke*, Alick Osborne. He made many trips as surgeon on convict ships and his skill can be reflected in the number of prisoners who made the long and arduous journey around the world successfully. In 1835 he decided to settle in Australia and took advantage of his job as surgeon on-board the convict ship *Marquis of Huntley* to bring his family along with him on the same ship. After settling in Australia he continued to act as surgeon on three more convict ships until he decided to become a farmer and took up the breeding of dairy cattle. It was during his time as a farmer at Newport, north of Sydney, that he fell victim to a gang of bushrangers called the Jewboy Gang. This band of outlaws had run wild in the whole of the area causing distress and mayhem with their violence and sacking of properties. During one of their rampaging forays they had made their way to Osborne's property where they took all that they wanted and threatened him using 'most provoking expressions'. It is ironic that the man who had made it his duty to help convicts had been so ill-used by them. Perhaps the life of a farmer was not for Osborne for he made his mark in Australian politics by becoming a Member of the Legislative Council for New South Wales in 1851, a post which he kept for four years until in 1856 he made his way to Ireland where, regretfully, this extremely well-travelled man died.

Transportation to Australia was a phenomenon that lasted for about 80 years, with the practice coming to an end in 1857. By that time, over 162,000 men, women and children from all over the Empire, with the vast majority from Britain, had been sent to do penal servitude in a new land on the far side of the world and not all of them were true criminals in the strictest sense of the word. Transportation had in the early stages been a kind of stopgap approach to the problem of housing criminals, a sort of out of sight, out of mind mentality, and it was not until a huge building programme was undertaken to construct modern prisons that the practice halted.

Back in England, the site of Lingard's gibbet had become a curiosity pointed out to all those willing to listen. Unlike Spence Broughton's remains, which had been on show for decades before they were finally removed, Lingard's had been on view for only 11 years until they were disposed of. The local landowners had complained bitterly about the disruption and damage caused by sightseers and had successfully petitioned for the removal of the remains, with some claiming that the sound of Lingard's bones rattling in the cage had kept them awake at night. Perhaps this excuse was just to stress the point about the gibbet being unwelcome. Many of his bones were buried beneath the gibbet itself by 'a cow doctor', while his skull was reputedly sent to Belle Vue in Manchester to be put on show as an exhibit in a curiosity museum or sideshow. After changing ownership more than once the skull that is alleged to be Lingard's is now on permanent display at the Littledean Jail in Gloucestershire. Even the smaller bones that were not buried became an object of desire, with one of the finger digits being reputedly turned into a pipe stopper. As for the gibbet and the irons there are a number of stories as to what became of these: the post is said to have been used as a beam in either a cottage or barn, with various buildings being described as the one concerned, while the irons in which Lingard was displayed were said to have been made into a variety of implements, probably as a memento of the occasion. Even though the majority of his bones were said to have been buried, the belief of the day stated that certain bones of an executed criminal held healing powers, so it is unlikely that he was 'all there' at the end.

William Bennett and William Lingard had both paid a high price for a moment of folly and had served many years of penal servitude in a far-off country, never returning home. After 21 years in custody William Bennett received his conditional pardon and the available evidence seems to show that he continued as a farmer in his chosen area, with his final years in Australia being a mystery.

William Lingard had to wait another five years to gain his freedom and his liberty when it came would have been a tremendous boost to his standing, but what became of him?

There is no mention of him at all in any of the records on Van Diemen's Land after the date of his pardon, so where did he go? The absence of any death records would imply that he left the island to travel elsewhere and that fits the history of the region for that time. In 1851 gold had been found near Bathurst in New South Wales and six months later there were several new strikes in the neighbouring state of Victoria. The Australian gold rushes had begun and anyone who wanted to make a quick killing was jumping on the bandwagon and heading into the outback. Many of those who tried their hands at prospecting were former convicts who saw the chance of an easy way to make a fortune and there is the possibility that William Lingard, using his new-found freedom, joined this band and made good. After all his trials and tribulations it would be nice to think so.

Lingard's home village of Litton and the countryside in which it sits have become one of the most beautiful areas of the whole country and the millions of tourists that visit it each year are free to come and go as they please, without the fear that was so prevalent all those years ago. As they travel around and see the sights do they realise just what happened in that one small corner of the Derbyshire Peaks when the two Lingards and Hannah Bocking brought so much misery and fear to it, and that Anthony Lingard became the last man ever to be gibbeted in Derbyshire? I doubt it. Nor do they realise that one small boy who suffered at the hands of an unscrupulous employer lived out the worst years of his life in that same area.

Robert Blincoe managed to complete his apprenticeship at Litton Mill in 1813 but his lack of training in any skilled work and the low wages that he had been paid meant that he had to stay at the mill for a further year. During this period he was able to save up a little money so that he could make a fresh start. After working at several other mills, where he felt that he was being exploited once more by having to work very long hours for small wages, he decided in 1817 to set up his own cotton business. At first his venture gave little reward for his efforts, yet gradually, both financially and personally, things improved and it was in 1819 that he met and married a woman by the name of Martha.

While Blincoe's fortunes had begun to improve, his former employer, Ellis Needham of Litton Mill, had hit hard times. In 1815, shortly after Blincoe had left the mill, Needham was declared bankrupt. His skills as a mill owner were poor and his gradual decline into complete insolvency was irreversible when in 1816 Lord Scarsdale cancelled the lease on his land. As a result of the closure of the mill scores of apprentices were made destitute and had to be kept by handouts from the parish.

As Ellis Needham's fortunes wavered and fell away, Robert Blincoe's continued to improve and it was in 1822 that he met John Brown, a journalist from Bolton, who interviewed him for an article about child labour that he was preparing. Brown was so taken by Blincoe's story that he passed his work to his friend Richard Carlile, the same Richard Carlile that had escaped from the Peterloo Massacre in 1819. Carlile was a radical newspaper owner, who was campaigning for new factory legislation and this was the type of information he was after. Sadly, John Brown committed suicide two or three years before his work came to print and that could have spelled the end for the story being published, for Carlile had done nothing with the article. Indeed, Carlile had difficulties of his own; this outspoken newspaper man had aroused the anger of the authorities by his constant publications demanding better conditions for workers and increased rights for women and would spend a total of 10 years in prison. It was not until 1828, after serving yet another prison sentence, that the biography of Robert Blincoe was published in Carlile's own newspaper *The Lion,* where it appeared in serial form over a period of five weeks from 25 January to 22 February. In this same year Blincoe's spinning machinery was destroyed in a fire, thereby putting him into financial difficulty and debt. Unable to continue making a living in the only profession he knew, he was imprisoned for not being able to clear his arrears. Following his release from prison he set up business as a cotton waste dealer and this time he made sure his project was a success, so much so he was able to pay for an education for his three children.

For all his efforts to help his fellow man, Richard Carlile ended his days in abject poverty and even after death he managed to stir up emotion among those around him. In a final gesture to help others, Carlile left his body to medical science and after the doctors had performed the necessary examinations his remains were taken for burial. At the funeral the clergyman began to deliver a graveside service much to the dismay of Carlile's children and the other mourners, for Carlile was an atheist and this would have been against his beliefs. The resultant commotion led to the children and some of the mourners leaving while the clergyman finished his words in defiance.

The year 1832 saw the publication of the pamphlet *A Memoir of Robert Blincoe, An Orphan Boy*. It was the story of Blincoe's early life and the times he had spent in the workhouse and mills and is believed by many to have been the basis for Charles Dickens's story of *Oliver Twist,* which first appeared in 1837.

Robert Blincoe lived on for some years until he died in 1860 as an old man, suffering from bronchitis, while staying at his daughter's house at Macclesfield. It is perhaps a fitting legacy that in the same year that the pamphlet containing his life story was produced he was requested to appear before the Employment of Children in Manufactories Committee. During the interview he was asked:

Have you any children?

Three.

Do you send them to factories?

## No. I would rather have them transported to Australia…

# APPENDIX A

William Newton was much affected by the sight of Anthony Lingard the elder watching his son's body after it was suspended from the gibbet and it had become a spectacle and a means of amusement for day-trippers and sightseers. This sight, combined with his knowledge of a letter written by Spence Broughton to his wife in 1792 as he waited to suffer the same fate that was to befall Lingard, inspired him to write this poem.

THE SUPPOSED SOLILOQUY OF A FATHER,
Under the Gibbet of his Son, upon one of the Peak mountains near Wardlow.
Time MIDNIGHT. Scene – A STORM.

ART thou, my Son, suspended here on high?
Ah! what a sight to meet a Father's eye!
To see what most I prized, what most I loved,
What most I cherish'd – and once most approved,
Hung in mid air to feed the nauseous worm,
And waving horrid in the midnight storm!

Let me be calm; – down, down, my swelling soul;
Ye winds, be still – ye thunders, cease to roll!
No! ye fierce winds, in all your fury rage;

Ye thunders, roll; ye elements, engage;
O'er me be all your mutual terrors spread,
And tear the thin hairs from your frenzied head:
Bring all your wrathful stores from either pole,
And strike your arrows through my burning soul:
I feel not – fear not – care not, shrink not – when
I know – believe – and feel – ye are not men;
Storms but fulfil the high decrees of God,
But man usurps his sceptre and His rod,
Tears from His hand the ensigns of His power,
To be the petty tyrant of an hour.

My son! My son! how dreadful was thy crime!
Thy name stands branded to remotest time;
Gives all thy kindred to the eye of scorn,
Both those who are, and those who may be born;
Scatters through ages of thy hapless race,
In every stage of life, and death, – disgrace:
In youth's gay prime, in manhood's perfect bloom –
Ah! more – it ends not, dies not, on the tomb!

O woman! woman! choicest blessing given,
If pure – the highest gift of highest heaven!
If lax, corrupt, deceitful – worse than hell!
Worse than the worst of demons dare to tell.
It was thy lot, ill fated son! to find

Thy doom pour'd on thee by the faithless kind;
Fraudful, and false their treacherous snares they spread,
And whelm'd destruction on thy thoughtless head.

To die, to perish from the face of earth,
Oblivion closing on thy name and birth,
Hid under ground from each invidious eye,
From every curious, very rancorous spy,
Was what thy crime deserv'd – not more;
The rest seems only cruelty. When heretofore
Our barbarous sires the awful Gibbet rear'd,
Gibbet only, not the laws were fear'd:
The untutor'd ruffian, of an untaught clime,
Fear'd more the punishment than dreaded crime.
We boast refinement, say our laws are mild,
Dealt equally to all, the man, the child:
But ye, who argue thus, come hear and see,
Feel with a Father's feelings – feel with me!
See that poor shrivell'd form the tempest brave,
See the red lightning strike, the waters lave,
The thunders volleying on that fenceless breast –
Who can see this, and wish him not at rest?

At rest – vague word! – the immaterial mind,
Perhaps even now is floating on the wind –
Ah! no – not mind – not spirit – but the shell;
The mind ere this has drank of Mercy's well.
'Tis not that I feel, for that I sigh,
But sweltering, putrid, rank mortality.
O! blind to truth, to all experience blind,
Who thinks such spectacles improve mankind;
Bid untamed youth on such sights feast his eyes,
Harden you may, but never humanise.
O ye who have life, or death, at your command,
Deal the sad dole, if death, with lenient hand,
If crime demands it, let the offender die,
But let no more the Gibbet brave the sky:
No more let vengeance on the dead be hurl'd,
But hide the victim from a gazing world.

# APPENDIX B

In 1792 Spence Broughton was tried and executed for robbing the mail, and it was this final, heartfelt letter to his wife written the night before he was to die that helped inspire William Newton to promote the abolition of gibbeting.

*York Castle,*
*April 14th 1792.*

*My Dear Eliza,*

*This is the last affectionate token thou wilt ever receive from my hand, a hand that trembles at my approaching desolation, so soon, so very soon to ensue, before thou wilt open this last epistle of thy unfortunate husband, these eyes, which now overflow with tears of contrition, shall have ceased to weep, and this heart now fluttering on the verge of eternity, shall beat no more; I have prepared my mind to meet death without fear, And ah how happy, had that been the common visitation of nature; Be not discomforted, God will be your friend, in the solitude of my cell I have sought him, and his spirit hath supported me, hath assisted me in my prayers, and many a time in the moments of remorseful anguish, hath whispered peace for my dear Eliza, I never added cruelty to injustice. Yet I have resolved to meet death without fear, one part of my awful sentence, a sentence aggravated by been merited, chills me with horror. When I reflect that my poor remains, the tokens of mortality, must not sleep, but be buffeted about by the storms of heaven, or parched by the summer's sun, while the traveller shrinks from them with disgust and terror. This consideration freezes my blood. This cell, this awful gloom, these irons, ye death itself is not grievous.Why will the laws continue to sport with the wretches after life is at an end. My Eliza – my friend – my wife, the last sad scene approaches, when I shall be no more, when I shall leave the world and thee my dear to as mercy, not only thee, but my unprotected children – the pledges of our love, through misfortune, through dissipation. Through vice and infamy, on thy part unchanged, oh fool that I was to think friendship could exist but with virtue, had I listened to the advice thou has so often given me, we had been a happy family respectable and respected. But it is past, that advice hath been slighted. I am doomed to an ignominious death and thou and my children horrid thought to infamy. To thee alone I trust the education of these illfated children, whom now more than ever I love and weep for, warn them against gaming of every description, that baleful vice which hath caused their father to be suspended a long and lasting spectacle, to feed the eyes of curiosity, teach them the way of religion in their early years, cause them to learn some trade, that business may fill their minds and leave no room for dissipation.When seated round your fire, when the little innocents enquire after their unfortunate father, tell them gaming was his ruin he neglected all religious duties he never conversed with his heart. In solitude he stifled the upbraiding of conscience in the company of the Lord and profligate, and is hung on high to after times I see thee employed while the tear trickles down that dear face I have so ill deserved. Adieu, my dear Eliza, adieu for ever the morning appears for the last time to these sad eyes.*

*Pleasant would death be on a sick bed after my soul had made a peace with God. With God I hope as peace is made he is not a God all terror. But a God all mercy, I rely on the interposition of a Saviour. May my tears, my penitence, my deep contrition be acceptedable to that Almighty being before whom I shall shortly have to appear. Adieu my Eliza adieu for ever; the pen falls from my hand slumber overtakes me the next will be the slumber of death.*

*Spence Broughton*

(Sheffield City Council Library Archives and Information: Sheffield Archives MD7337/1/1–2)

To our eyes the spelling and grammar are somewhat erratic and indeed to make it more comprehensible small liberties have been taken with the spelling and punctuation to make it more readable, yet still the love that Broughton feels for his wife Eliza and the thought of his future plight comes through with feeling.

# APPENDIX C

It was tradition for convicted criminals who were sentenced to death to confess their guilt and to give out a warning to others not to follow them on the path to self-destruction. Many of these so-called 'confessions of guilt' were at least partly fabricated by newspapers and publishers to show that the right person was to hang and that a miscarriage of justice had not taken place. Three days before his execution Spence Broughton asked for pen, ink and paper and wrote this heartfelt plea, not to other would-be lawbreakers, but to God as a plea for his soul.

*Surely I have greatly transgressed the laws both of God and man! In what manner shall a sinful wretch, like me, presume to approach the throne of mercy? Alas! my repeated provocation do now wound to the very soul. How have I trifled away the hours, the days, the months and the years of my life! O the profligacy of my heart! O the misery that I have, as it were laboured to bring forth! Father of mercies forgive me. Jesus my Saviour, plead for me, for, if thou inclinest thine ear, I am eternally happy; otherwise eternally miserable. To thee I commend my soul…O take it to thy heavenly protection! So shall I pass thro' the vale [sic] of stars, to the heaven of perfect and uninterrupted blessedness. Grant me, gracious God this heartfelt, dying request, and I will not be dismayed; for thou alone art a refuge for those who confide in thee.*

# APPENDIX D

In 1819 Thomas Hopkinson was executed at Derby for highway robbery after falling foul of his accomplice, John Fletcher, who turned King's evidence in order to save his own life. While in gaol Hopkinson bemoaned the fact that he himself had done the same two years previously instead of admitting to horse stealing, which would have given him a sentence of transportation for 14 years and would have stopped him from sinking further into a criminal life. While in Chesterfield gaol waiting to be taken to Derby he made a confession to W.A. Lord listing all his known crimes:

Cutting at five different times horses' manes and tails and two cows' tails.

Cutting off the hind feet of a live sheep in the turnpike road.

Two highway robberies.

Breaking into butchers' shops at three different times and stealing thereout whole sides and joints of mutton.

Breaking into one house, one shop, one pantry, two corn mills, and one turnpike house, and stealing thereout flour, meal, meat, etc.

Robbing gardens of cabbage plants and other vegetables, fruit etc 27 times.

Stealing one poney (sic).

Stealing at 95 different times, 209 fowls, 21 geese, nine ducks, and four turkies (sic).

Stealing at 32 different times, 65 pecks of wheat.

Stealing at 20 different times, 72 rabbits.

Stealing at 20 different times, 112 pecks of potatoes.

Stealing at 20 different times, 18 sheep and three lambs and skinning one alive.

Milking cows in the night belonging to 66 different persons.

Stealing at four different times, 108 pigeons out of dovecotes.

Setting fire to corn stacks and attempting to fire others, and stealing at different periods one dog, five game cocks, two scythes, two hay rakes, one pair of cotton stockings, two beehives, one smockfrock, one oak plank, two pewter pints, two brass pans, two copper tea kettles, one metal pot, 1lb candles, hay, yarn, horse hair, coal, sack bags, 18 cheeses, barley, oats, taking from a child, 2s 6d, and from another child, one and a half stone of flour etc.

Hopkinson had taken to a life of crime at the age of 14 and was only 20 years old when he was executed.

# APPENDIX E

The 1828 census of New South Wales shows that William Carter employed many convicts on his farm including William Bennett. Carter was a free settler – in other words he was in Australia as a matter of choice and not as a convict. There is little doubt that he was one of those who saw an opportunity to make a fresh start and a lot of money in a new land that was being opened up. His census entry states that his was a free farm with 9,000 acres, while the entries for those he employed lists their names, convict ship on which they were transported and the role in which they were employed. Carter would have paid very low wages if any at all to his convict labour.

| William Hatson | *Archduke Charles* | employed by Carter |
| Isaac Holmes | *Granada* | fencer employed by Carter |
| Henry Hone | *Adamant* | employed by Carter |
| John Lynch | *Brampton* | employed by Carter |
| Patrick McCarthy | *Dorothy Shepherd* | assigned servant |
| Alexandre McDougall | *Countess of Harcourt* | shepherd assigned servant |
| Edward Williams | *Fanny* | assigned servant |
| Caroline Williams | *Mariner* | assigned servant |
| John Sadlier | *Asia* | employed by Carter |
| George Frankham | *Pheonix* | drayman assigned servant |
| Edward Johnson | *Mangles* | shepherd assigned servant |
| Mary Ahern | *Elizabeth* | servant |

| | | |
|---|---|---|
| **William Bennett** | *Speke* | **servant** |
| Anthony Boland | *Marquis of Huntley* | servant |
| James Brogan | *Marquis of Huntley* | servant |
| John Butler | *Mangles* | servant |
| Richard Clarke | *Lord Eldon* | employed by Carter |
| Richard Clayburn | *Guildford* | servant |
| George Wiggledon | *Earl St Vincent* | employed by Carter |
| William Williams | *Countess of Harcourt* | servant |
| William Dean, painter | *Countess of Harcourt* | servant |
| Joseph Duick | | employed by Carter |
| Phillip Eaton | *Bussorah Merchant* | shepherd assigned servant |
| Dennis Fitzgerald | *Guildford* | watchman assigned servant |
| Christopher Flood | | employed by Carter |
| John Green | *John Barry* | sawyer employed by Carter |

Out of 26 people employed on William Carter's farm only two were free settlers or convicts who had completed their terms and had opted to stay in Australia, the rest were prisoners assigned to him so that they could fulfil a useful purpose. Carter did not always have it his own way though, for in the early 1830s a W. Carter lost a court case over some disputed land and later appeared in court over outstanding bills. It is probable that Carter lost some or all of his farm and this could be why Bennett was later recorded as working for Harley Grayson of Dungog. It is worth taking note of the names of the convict ships that were used to transport Carter's workers to Australia and to bear in mind that this is only a tiny selection of those used.

# NOTES

1.  Anna Seward (1747–1809) was born in nearby Eyam and moved to Litchfield as a young girl. She became a well-respected writer and mixed with the literary figures of the day. When visited by Samuel Johnson and James Boswell she declined to have much to do with either of them and instead preferred the company of people like Erasmus Darwin (the grandfather of Charles Darwin) and other such intellectuals. In later life she corresponded with Sir Walter Scott, and although she is mainly forgotten nowadays, she was highly thought of in her own time and was given the epithet of 'The Swan of Litchfield'.

2.  To read the full poem see Appendix A.

3.  For the full text of this letter see Appendix B.

4.  See Appendix D.

5.  See Appendix E.

# SELECTED BIBLIOGRAPHY

**Abbott, Geoffrey** *Lords of the Scaffold* Dobby Publishing, Orpington, 2001.

**Ash, Russell** *Discovering Highwaymen* Shire Publications, 1994.

**Briggs, John, Christopher Harrison, Angus McInnes and David Vincent** *Crime and Punishment in England* UCL Press, London 2001.

**Brooke, Alan and David Brandon** *Bound for Botany Bay. British Convict Voyages to Australia* The National Archives, 2005.

**Brooke, Alan and David Brandon** *Tyburn. London's Fatal Tree* Sutton Publishing, Stroud, 2004.

**Brown, John** *A Memoir of Robert Blincoe* Richard Carlile, London, 1832.

**Campbell, Charles** *The Intolerable Hulks. British Shipboard Confinement 1776–1857* Heritage Books, Maryland, USA, 1994.

**Cawthorne, Nigel** *Public Executions From Ancient Rome to the Present Day* Arcturus, London, 2006.

**Cox, J. Charles** *The Churches of Derbyshire* Vol 2 Bemrose and Sons, London, 1876.

**Cox, Revd Charles** *Three Centuries of Derbyshire Annals* Vol 2 London, 1860.

**Daniels, Clarence** *Pinnacles of Peak History* 1947.

**Foss, Edward** *The Judges of England, Vol IX* John Murray, London, 1864.

**Garner, Edward** *Hanged for Three Pennies* Breedon Books, Derby, 2000.

**Glover** *History and Gazetteer of the County of Derby* Vol 2 1833.

**Haining, Peter** *The English Highwayman. A Legend Unmasked* Robert Hale, London, 1991.

**Hill, C.P.** *British Economic and Social History 1700–1964* Edward Arnold, Bristol, 1974.

**Hithens, Peter** *A Brief History of Crime. The Decline of Order, Justice and Liberty in England* Atlantic Books, London, 2003.

**Jay, Mike** *The Unfortunate Colonel Despard* Bantam, London, 2004.

**Lugard, C.E.** *The Saints and Sinners and the Inns and Outs of Ashover* 1924.

**Mayhew, Henry and John Binney** *The Criminal Prisons of London and Scenes of London Life* 1862.

**Morgan, Kenneth O. (ed)** *History of Britain 1789–1983* OUP, London, 1985.

**Picard, Liza** *Restoration London* Phoenix, London, 1997.

**Rhodes, Ebenezer** *Peak Scenery* 1824.

**Taylor, David** *Crime, Policing and Punishment in England, 1750–1914* MacMillan, London, 1998.

**Thornhill, Robert (ed)** *A Village Constables Accounts 1791–1839* 1957.

**White, Charles** *Convict Life in New South Wales and Van Diemen's Land* 1889.

# OTHER SELECTED SOURCES

Australian Medical Pioneers Index

*Derby Mercury* 1815–26

*Derbyshire Life*

*Derbyshire Miscellany* Vol 6, Part 1, 1971

Derbyshire Records Office (Archives), Parish Records

Derby Local Studies Library, Broadsheets and Calendar of Prisoners

Hansard. HC deb 13 March 1834 Vol 22

New South Wales Department of Commerce State Records

Tasmanian State Archives

Society of Australian Genealogists

State Library of New South Wales

The Newgate Calendar

*Whites Directory* 1857

ND - #0279 - 270225 - C0 - 172/110/14 - PB - 9781780911700 - Gloss Lamination